LETTERS FR~~OM BU~~

Aung San Suu Kyi is the leader of the struggle for human rights and democracy in Burma. Born in 1945 as the daughter of Burma's national hero Aung San, she was two years old when he was assassinated, just before Burma gained the independence to which he had dedicated his life. After receiving her education in Rangoon, Delhi and at Oxford University, Aung San Suu Kyi then worked at the United Nations in New York and Bhutan. For most of the following twenty years she was occupied raising a family in England (her husband is British), before returning to Burma in 1988 to care for her dying mother. Her return coincided with the outbreak of a spontaneous revolt against twenty-six years of political repression and economic decline. Aung San Suu Kyi ('Suu' to her friends and family) quickly emerged as the most effective and articulate leader of the movement, and the party she founded went on to win a colossal electoral victory in May 1990. In July 1989 she was put under house arrest and the military junta that now rules Burma refused for six years either to free her or to transfer power to a civilian government as it had promised. Upon her release in July 1995 she immediately resumed the struggle for political freedom in her country.

Aung San Suu Kyi is an honorary fellow of St Hugh's College, Oxford. In 1990 she was awarded the Thorolf Rafto Prize for Human Rights in Norway and the Sakharov Prize for Freedom of Thought by the European Parliament, and in 1991 she was awarded the Nobel Peace Prize. In its citation the Norwegian Nobel Committee stated that in awarding the Prize to Aung San Suu Kyi, it wished 'to honour this woman for her unflagging efforts and to show its support for the many people throughout the world who are striving to attain democracy, human rights and ethnic conciliation by peaceful means'.

Aung San Suu Kyi is also author of several books, including *Freedom from Fear*, which was edited by her husband, Dr Michael Aris, and *The Voice of Hope*, both of which are published by Penguin.

Fergal Keane, OBE, is one of the BBC's most distinguished correspondents and has been named reporter of the year on television and radio. His books are *The Bondage of Fear*, *Season of Blood*, winner of the 1995 Orwell Prize, and *Letter to Daniel*, all published by Penguin.

LETTERS
FROM BURMA

Aung San Suu Kyi

Illustrated by Heinn Htet

INTRODUCTION BY FERGAL KEANE

PENGUIN BOOKS

PENGUIN BOOKS

Published by the Penguin Group
Penguin Books Ltd, 27 Wrights Lane, London w8 5TZ, England
Penguin Books USA Inc., 375 Hudson Street, New York, New York 10014, USA
Penguin Books Australia Ltd, Ringwood, Victoria, Australia
Penguin Books Canada Ltd, 10 Alcorn Avenue, Toronto, Ontario, Canada M4V 3B2
Penguin Books (NZ) Ltd, 182–190 Wairau Road, Auckland 10, New Zealand

Penguin Books Ltd, Registered Offices: Harmondsworth, Middlesex, England

First published as *Biruma Kara no tegami (Letters form Burma)* by Mainichi Shinbunsha, 1996
Published in Penguin Books 1997
1 3 5 7 9 10 8 6 4 2

Extract from *The Waste Land* by kind permission of Faber and Faber Ltd, from
Collected Poems 1909–1962 by T. S. Eliot.
From the Morning of the World: Poems from the Manyoshu, translated from the Japanese by
Graeme Wilson. First published in Great Britain in 1991 by Harvill. © Graeme Wilson, 1991.
Reproduced by permission of The Harvill Press.

Set in 10/13pt Monotype Garamond
Typeset by Rowland Phototypesetting Ltd, Bury St Edmunds, Suffolk
Printed in England by Clays Ltd, St Ives plc

Contents

Introduction

by Fergal Keane

On the morning of my ninth wedding anniversary I found myself unexpectedly rushing to catch a Thai Airways flight to Rangoon, the Burmese capital. The plane was crowded with journalists who had heard, like me, that the Burmese opposition leader Aung San Suu Kyi had been released from house arrest after six years. I was preparing to enter the country on a tourist visa, having been told by Burma's representatives in Hong Kong that I would have to wait several days for an official journalist's permit. Thus as our plane came in over Rangoon, and I saw the still-flooded paddies beyond the city and the first golden temples, I was preoccupied with simply getting into the country and getting out fast with the story. At that stage I knew little about the internal politics of Burma or its history. Like everybody else on the aircraft I was frantically reading the news clippings about Aung San Suu Kyi and her jailers, the State Law and Order Restoration Council or SLORC as they are known and dreaded by the Burmese people. What I quickly gleaned was that Aung San Suu Kyi was not merely the leader of the opposition. In actual fact she was the leader of the party which had won more than 80 per cent of the seats contested in an election called by the military back in 1990. This election took place a year after the army had shot many thousands of unarmed demonstrators and while Aung San Suu Kyi was under house arrest. Her National League for Democracy had been forced to campaign without its leader but had still managed to win a huge victory.

I had of course seen news reports about Burma on television and had frequently seen Aung San Suu Kyi's photograph in the newspapers. The photographs had been taken while she was at liberty, in the months when she travelled the length and breadth of Burma rallying the people behind the NLD. The word 'charismatic' was used a great deal by those who wrote about her. One of the stories told of how she had faced down an army officer who had given his men orders to shoot her. She had simply continued walking calmly down the road until another officer intervened and countermanded the order. But colleagues who visited Burma in more recent times warned me that the country was blanketed by a state of fear. People would not talk to journalists. The government's spies were everywhere. Telephone lines were unsafe and those who had attempted to approach Aung San Suu Kyi's home on University Avenue had been roughly sent on their way by soldiers. As it happened, the atmosphere in Rangoon was considerably more relaxed on the afternoon I arrived. There were no problems at immigration or customs. A couple of thuggish-looking types wearing shades lurked around the entrance to the airport but they paid no attention to me. They were clearly waiting for somebody else.

Bearing in mind the warnings about spies, I kept the conversation with the taxi driver to a minimum of bland platitudes. A lovely country, I agreed. Pretty scenery. And then the driver noticed the paper I was carrying. On the front page of the *Bangkok Post* was a large picture of Aung San Suu Kyi. The driver smiled and said to himself: 'The Lady, the Lady.' 'You like her?' I enquired. 'We don't like her, sir, we love her,' he replied. Thus was I introduced to the powerful affection which the ordinary people of Burma feel for Aung San Suu Kyi. It is a feeling which prompts thousands of them to risk their lives and physical freedom by attending rallies outside her home each weekend. I have asked numerous people – teachers, peasants, monks, even a few off-duty soldiers – why there is such a well-spring of feeling for Aung San Suu Kyi. After all, she has been actively involved at the forefront of Burmese politics for less than a decade – nothing like the lifetime of political struggle of her fellow Nobel laureate Nelson Mandela. Perhaps the most eloquent answer to my question came from an old man, standing drenched to the skin outside Aung San Suu Kyi's house on the day after her release. 'We come here because we know that we are the most important thing in the world to her. She cares about us.' To a people who suffer continually the brutality of one of the world's most odious regimes, the notion that a leader might actually care about them, and risk her own freedom to fight for theirs, is indeed unusual.

Later, when I came to meet Aung San Suu Kyi and we became friends, I began to appreciate the singular qualities which inspired such devotion among her followers. Chief among the attributes which make her a remarkable leader in our times is a deep humanity, a gift for understanding and embracing the pain of others as if it were her own. Much of her time these days is spent listening to the voices of ordinary people, who risk arrest by coming to her compound to talk about their problems. Poverty, military oppression, the hunger for arable land, all are discussed with the supplicants who come to the house by the lake. None are turned away without being given a hearing. Now reading these wonderful letters from Burma, written between November 1995 and December 1996, in the few spare moments she has managed to find away from public life, I am again touched by the sense of decency which shines through. In a world so massively consumed by greed and hatred, her plea for a simpler and more person-centred politics is breathtakingly refreshing. In one of her letters she writes:

Some have questioned the appropriateness of talking about such matters as *metta* (loving-kindness) and *thissa* (truth) in the political context. But politics is about people and what we had seen . . . proved that love and truth can move people more strongly than any form of coercion.

Many of the letters are of course strongly political. How could they be otherwise? With Burma in the grip of despotic rule, with thousands of her supporters in prison, and countless more of Burma's people being forced to work on slave-labour projects, some of the letters make harrowing reading. Her descriptions of prison conditions and the plight of the children of prisoners induce feelings of sorrow and outrage. Having been forcibly separated from her own children by the regime, Aung San Suu Kyi writes with an intimate knowledge of her subject. There is not however a trace of self-pity and there is always a sense of joyous engagement with the world. These writings are always informed by her own personal experience or the life-stories of friends and family or the countless visitors to her compound. For example, when writing about the need for health care and education in Burma she paints a beautiful word-picture of the arrival of a close friend's new grandchild.

She remained resolutely asleep even when I picked her up and we all clustered around to have our photograph taken with the new star in our firmament . . . Certainly I like both the shape and smell of babies, but I wonder whether their attraction does not lie in something more than merely physical attributes. Is it not the thought of a life stretching out like a shining clean slate on which might one day be written the most beautiful prose and poetry of existence, that engenders such joy in the hearts of the parents and grandparents of a newly born child?

As can be seen from the above, this is not a book of tedious political cant. The sights, smells and tastes of Burma are all here as well as Aung San Suu Kyi's warm sense of humour. Accompanied by the beautiful line drawings of Heinn Htet, you can read letters about, among other things, the national habit of tea-drinking; the struggle to repair the leaky roof of her house; a reflection on some of her favourite poetry; a hilarious dissertation on the eating habits of the principal characters in the spy and detective novels which she still loves to read. For example, writing about the private eye Nero Wolfe, she says:

It was because of this obese private investigator's fulsome praise of the chicken fricassee with dumplings he ate at a church fête that I learnt to cook that deliciously homely dish.

A strong spiritual theme runs through her letters. As a devout Buddhist Aung San Suu Kyi spends a proportion of each day in prayer and meditation. The story of her visit to the Thamanya Sayadaw – the most revered Buddhist monk in the country – is painted with particular skill and sensitivity. I regard such writing as evidence of a unique combination in modern leadership: a fiercely active mind and a warm, forgiving spirit. When most other politicians talk about morality one is tempted to throw one's eyes up to heaven. Rarely does their behaviour match up to rhetoric. But when Aung San Suu Kyi talks about a spiritual revolution nobody sneers, except perhaps the dark generals of SLORC, for whom the gun and the torture cell are the ultimate weapons of politics. Yet even for them she has capacity for compassion. Nowhere in these letters is there any sense of bitterness. Tough and forthright criticism yes, but not a trace of vengefulness. In her public speeches she has always taken care to speak the language of reconciliation. Her private views are exactly the same. Many people ask whether such idealism could survive the test of being in government with all the tough decisions and compromises such office demands. I believe the answer to that question can be found in the character of Aung San Suu Kyi, particularly as reflected in these pages.

Here is a woman who has already made some of the toughest decisions imaginable. At any time since her house arrest she could have taken an easy way out and left Burma to live in England with husband and sons. Instead she made a painful personal sacrifice, placing her belief in freedom and the love of her country first. She lives with the knowledge that just as SLORC has locked up and 'disappeared' many of her closest friends and associates, so too is it capable of doing the same to her at any time. Yet she chooses to stay on and continue with her non-violent struggle for freedom. I have heard some people say that Aung San Suu Kyi is 'tough'. I prefer to use the word 'strong'. This is not the strength of guns or money but rather the power derived from faith in a simple idea: that all men and women have the right to a life that is free from fear and oppression. Were she to be allowed to take her rightful place as the elected leader of the Burmese people, I have little doubt that the principles so eloquently expressed in these pages would illuminate her governance. This is a book to be savoured and cherished. It is of course extremely well-written, but more than that, it offers us a privileged encounter with one of the most remarkable leaders of our time. Read it and revel in the courage, the strength and the humanity.

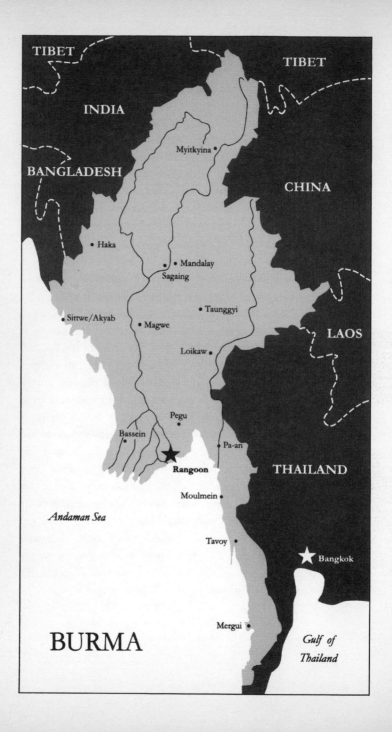

LETTERS FROM BURMA

1. The Road to Thamanya (1)

Twenty miles from the town of Pa-an in the Karen State is a hill that was known to the Mon people in ancient times as 'Paddy Seed Hill' because it resembled a heap of paddies. The Karen and Pa-o peoples who lived in the surrounding villages would go up the hill to chop wood and to bake charcoal. Often they met with strange experiences which made them observe that this was not a '*thamanya*' (in Pali, *samanyal* meaning 'ordinary') place. With one of those perverse twists of linguistic logic, the hill came to be known as Thamanya.

In 1980 the Venerable U Vinaya, a 69-year-old Buddhist monk of Pa-o extraction, went up the hill to the site of two ruined pagodas that had stood at the summit for centuries. Stirred by feelings of deep devotion the ageing monk decided to remain near the site of the long neglected pagodas. Now, fifteen years later, the extraordinary 'ordinary' hill of Thamanya is known throughout Burma as a famous place of pilgrimage, a sanctuary ruled by the *metta* (loving-kindness) of the *Hsayadaw*, the holy teacher, U Vinaya.

Two weeks ago I made a trip outside Rangoon for the first time since my release from house arrest. A party of us set out in three cars at four o'clock in the morning along the road to Pegu in the north-east. We were headed for Thamanya, to pay our respects to the *Hsayadaw* and to receive his blessings. There is a special charm to journeys undertaken before daybreak in hot lands: the air is soft and cool and the coming of dawn reveals a landscape fresh from the night dew. By the time it was light enough for us to see beyond the headlights of our car, we had left the outskirts of Rangoon behind us. The road was bordered by fields dotted with palms and every now and then in the distance could be seen the white triangle of a *stupa* wreathed in morning mist, tipped with a metal 'umbrella' that glinted reddish gold in the glow of the rising sun.

I was travelling in a borrowed Pajero: the young men in our party assured me that this was the best kind of car for rough country. They said successive safari rallies had been won by a Pajero. I think there must have been a bit of difference between those triumphant Pajeros and the one in which we went to Thamanya. Our vehicle was old and in an indifferent state of repair, and every time we hit a particularly rough spot there would be a vigorous and unpredictable reaction. Several times a light that did not normally work switched itself on abruptly; the car radio dropped off and could not be put back; a thermos flask full of hot water exploded in protest; a first-aid box which we had thought securely ensconced at the back was suddenly found nestling against my feet. I had to keep myself from bouncing too far towards the roof by holding on grimly to the headrests of the front seats. There were times when it felt as though I was perpetually suspended in mid-air.

At about six o'clock in the morning we drove through Pegu. Once it was a capital city of the Mons and also of King Bayinnaung, the one Burmese monarch who left the heartland to settle in the south, demonstrating a rare interest in the world beyond the confines of his original home. Nowadays Pegu no longer has a royal air, but it is still graced by the Shwemawdaw Pagoda and by a huge reclining image of the Buddha, the Shwethalyaung.

The road had become worse as we travelled further and further away from Rangoon. In compensation the landscape became more beautiful. Our eyes rejoiced at rural Burma in all its natural glory even though our bones were jolted as our car struggled to negotiate the dips and craters in the road. Fortunately, all of us shared a keen sense of humour and the violent bumps seemed to us more comic than painful. Between rising into the air and landing back with resounding thuds on our seats we managed to admire the scenery: the tender green of the graceful paddy plants; the beautiful lotuses, pink, white and blue, floating in pools and ditches; the dark, violet-washed hills carved into rolling shapes that conjured up images of fairy-tale creatures; the sky shading from pale turquoise to bright azure, streaked with deceptively still banks of clouds; the picturesque thatch huts perched on slender wooden poles, sometimes half-hidden behind delicate bamboo fences trailing a frieze of flowering plant. But these pretty habitations lacked comfort, and the people who lived there were very poor.

Around eight o'clock we crossed the Sittang bridge into the Mon State. Passing through the small towns of Kyaik-hto and Kyaik-kaw we saw the signboards of the National League for Democracy (NLD) gallantly displayed in front of extremely modest little offices. These signboards, brilliantly red and white, are a symbol of the courage of people who have remained dedicated to their beliefs in the face of severe repression, whose commitment to democracy has not been shaken by the adversities they have experienced. The thought that such people are to be found all over Burma lifted my heart.

2. The Road to Thamanya (2)

The country we had been going through was rocky. At Mokpalin we had passed a rock quarry where, I was told, convicts were usually to be seen working. We saw none on our way to Thamanya, but on our way back we were to see two men in white with chains on their legs trotting along the roadway, shouldering a pole from which hung large baskets full of broken rock.

In the vicinity of Kyaik-hto is the Kyaik-htiyoe pagoda. It is only fifteen feet in height but it is one of the most famous religious monuments in Burma because it is built on a large skull-shaped rock amazingly balanced on the edge of a jutting crag 3600 feet above sea level. Its perch is so precarious that the push of one strong man can set it rocking gently. Yet it has managed to maintain its equilibrium over many centuries.

There are rubber plantations all along the route from the Sittang bridge until the town of Thaton, a straggled out place with a slightly battered air. When we were schoolchildren we were taught that rubber was one of the main export products of Burma. But over the last few decades our rubber industry gradually declined and now rubber no longer features among our important natural assets.

Once upon a time Thaton with its twilight air was a thriving capital and a famous centre for Buddhism, ruled over by the Mon King Manuha, a monarch who commanded the respect of friend and foe alike. Although he was defeated in battle and carried away as a captive by King Anawratha of Pagan, Manuha's personal stature remained undiminished. Popular Burmese history has it that even in defeat his glory was so manifest, that every time Manuha made obeisance to Anawratha, the victor king broke out into a sweat of fear. In the end,

7

it is said, Anawratha managed to destroy Manuha's glory by underhand means.

In Pagan today there still remains the Manuha *stupa* with a dedication by the captive king praying that he might never again, in any of his future lives, be defeated. The sympathetic account of King Manuha is one of the most admirable parts of Burmese history, demonstrating a lack of ethnic prejudice and unstinting respect for a noble enemy.

From Thaton we continued to travel in an easterly direction and at about eleven o'clock we entered the Karen State. The state capital Pa-an lies on the east bank of the river Salween which we crossed by car ferry. Pa-an is a spacious town, quiet and pleasantly countrified. We did not stop there at this time, as we had made arrangements to meet members of the Karen State NLD later, on the way back from Thamanya.

There is an untamed beauty about the lands around Pa-an. The area is notable for its striking hills that rise sheer from the ground. In some of the hills are caves in which old Mon inscriptions, images and pagodas have been found. It was in one of these caves that a queen of Manuha took refuge after the defeat of her husband. It is believed that this queen later moved, for greater security, to the foot of 'Paddy Seed Hill' and that it was she who had the two pagodas constructed on its summit.

As we approached Thamanya, the quiet seemed to deepen. It was difficult to imagine that we were close to areas which have served as battlefields over most of the last fifty years. Fighting broke out between government troops and Karen insurgents almost as soon as Burma was declared an independent nation in January 1948. And there has not yet been a political settlement that could bring permanent peace to this land with its wild, magical quality.

The *Hsayadaw* of Thamanya is a vegetarian and only vegetarian food is served in his domain. It is customary for those making the journey to Thamanya to start eating vegetarian food at least the day before they set out. We too had been eating vegetarian food and we felt full of health and calm self-satisfaction as we covered the last lap of our journey. Suddenly it occurred to us that the quietness and ease had to do with something more than the beauties of nature or our state of mind. We realized that the road had become less rough. Our vehicle was no longer leaping from crater to rut and we were no longer rolling around the car like peas in a basin.

As soon as we passed under the archway that marked the beginning of the domain of Thamanya, the road became even better: a smooth, well-kept black ribbon winding into the distance. The difference between the road we had been travelling on and this one struck all of us. This road had been built and maintained by the *Hsayadaw* for the convenience of the villagers who lived around the hill and of the pilgrims who came in their tens of thousands each year. It was far superior to many a highway to be found in Rangoon.

3. At Thamanya (1)

It was noon when we entered the three-mile radius around the hill of Thamanya that comes under the fatherly care of the *Hsayadaw*. The air hung warm and still and groups of monks, women ascetics and little novices were working on the road, the end of their robes draped over their shaven heads, their faces well-rounded and cheerful. We passed clusters of huts and small bungalows smothered in tangles of greenery, and at last came up through a bazaar to the foot of the hill where there were some brick buildings and a number of cars. It was not too crowded. Soon, after the full moon of *Thidingyut*, the place would be bustling with thousands of pilgrims from all over the country. We had deliberately chosen to come at a time when we could listen quietly to the *Hsayadaw* and absorb the spirit of this unusual domain of loving-kindness and peace founded on the edge of lands where violence had held sway for decades.

The *Hsayadaw* divides his time between two monastic residences, one at the foot of the hill and one near the summit. He received us in the audience chamber of the residence at the foot of the hill. I am about to describe the *Hsayadaw* as tall and well-built, then my eyes fall on his photograph and it occurs to me that he was not physically as large as the image impressed on my mind, that in fact he was somewhat frail. Perhaps it was the aura of protective strength around him that made him seem bigger than he actually was. There is a Burmese saying: 'Ten thousand birds can perch on one good tree.' The *Hsayadaw* is a strong, upright tree spreading out stout branches thickly covered with leaves and laden with fruit, offering shelter and sustenance to all who come under his shade.

On and around the hill which was barely inhabited little more than a decade ago there now live over 400 monks and between 200 and 300 women ascetics, all cared for by the *Hsayadaw*. In addition, everybody who comes to the hill can eat flavoursome vegetarian meals without any payment. Many of the villagers who live within the domain come daily for their food. On holidays when pilgrims flood in, more than sixty sacks of rice have to be cooked and almost a whole drum of oil goes into the curries. The *Hsayadaw* is very particular about using only peanut oil in the interest of the health of his hordes of visitors.

There is a large shed in which twenty men cook rice in giant steamers made of concrete. In the kitchen, appetizing-looking curries bubble and simmer in huge wok-shaped vessels; the spoons, carved out of wood, are larger than shovels and the spatulas used for stirring are as big as rowing-boat oars. Not far from the kitchen some people are engaged in making meat substitute from a type of yam. It is not difficult to be a vegetarian at Thamanya: the food, cooked with generosity and care, is both wholesome and delicious. The day of our arrival we had two lunches, one specially prepared for us and one in the pilgrims' dining hall. The second lunch consisted of just a few dishes but these were not inferior in taste to the banquet-like meal we had first eaten and replete as we were, we found it no hardship to do justice to the food of the pilgrims.

But food is not primarily what the *Hsayadaw* provides for those who come within his ken. The first question he asked me after we had made our obeisances was whether I had come to him because I wanted to get rich. No, I replied, I was not interested in getting rich. He went on to explain that the greatest treasure to be gained was that of *nirvana*. How naïve I was to have imagined that the *Hsayadaw* would have been referring to material riches. He spoke in parables to teach us the fundamental principles of Buddhism. But there was nothing affected about him and his deeply spiritual nature did not exclude a sense of humour.

The *Hsayadaw* seldom leaves Thamanya but he displays astonishing knowledge of all that is going on throughout the country. He combines traditional Buddhist values with a forward-looking attitude, and is prepared to make use of modern technology in the best interests of those who have come under his care. There are a number of strong, useful cars in Thamanya that the *Hsayadaw*'s active young monk assistants use to go dashing around the domain checking on road-construction projects.

The *Hsayadaw* himself also goes out every day (driven in a Pajero donated by one of his devotees, vastly superior to our borrowed vehicle) to encourage the workers and to give them snacks, *pan* (a preparation of betel leaf, lime and areca nuts) and cheroots. The sight of his serene face and this tangible proof of his concern for them seems to spur on the workers to greater efforts.

Whenever the *Hsayadaw* goes through his domain people sink down on their knees in obeisance, their faces bright with joy. Young and old alike run out of their homes as soon as they spot his car coming, anxious not to miss the opportunity of receiving his blessing.

4. At Thamanya (2)

On our second day at Thamanya we rose at three o'clock in the morning: we wanted to serve the *Hsayadaw* his first meal of the day, which he takes at four o'clock. We had expected that we would all be suffering from the after-effects of the cavorting of the Pajero but in fact we had all slept extremely well and suffered from no aches or pains.

When we stepped out into the street it was still dark. Going out before dawn had been a constant feature of the campaign trips I had undertaken between the autumn of 1988 and the time when I was placed under house arrest. But I have never ceased to be moved by the sense of the world lying quiescent and vulnerable, waiting to be awakened by the light of the new day quivering just beyond the horizon.

The *Hsayadaw* had spent the night at his residence on the hill and when we went up he came out of his small bedroom, his face clear and his eyes bright. With a glowing smile he spoke of the importance of looking upon the world with joy and sweetness. After we had served the *Hsayadaw* his breakfast, we went to offer lights at the twin pagodas on the summit of the hill. On the platform around the pagodas were a few people who had spent the whole night there in prayer. There is a beauty about candlelight that cannot be equalled by the most subtle electric lamps; and there is an immense satisfaction about setting the flames of fifty white candles dancing, creating a blazing patch of brightness in the grey of early morning. It was an auspicious start to the working day.

I had expressed an interest in seeing the two schools within the domain of Thamanya and after breakfast (another vegetarian banquet) we were greatly surprised and honoured to learn that the *Hsayadaw* himself would be taking us to look at the institutions. He is very conscious of the importance of education and arranges for pupils to be brought in by bus from the outlying areas. First we went to the middle school at Wekayin village. It is a big rickety wooden building on stilts and the whole school assembled on the beaten earth floor between the stilts to pay their respects to the *Hsayadaw*, who distributed roasted beans to everybody. The 375 children are taught by thirteen teachers struggling with a dearth of equipment. The headmaster is a young man with an engaging directness of manner who talked, without the slightest trace of self-pity or discouragement, about the difficulties of acquiring even such basic materials as textbooks. Of course the situation of Wekayin middle school is no different from that of schools all over Burma but it seemed especially deserving of assistance because of the dedication of the teachers and the happy family atmosphere.

The elementary school is in Thayagone village. On our way there we stopped to pick up some children who sat in our car demurely with suppressed glee on their faces, clutching their bags and lunch boxes. When we reached the school they tumbled out merrily and we followed them along a picturesque lane overhung with flowering climbers. The school itself is a long, low bungalow, smaller than the middle school, and there are only three teachers in charge of 230 pupils. As at Wekayin, roasted beans were distributed and the little ones munched quietly away while the *Hsayadaw* told us of his plans to replace both schools with more solid brick buildings and we discussed ways and means of providing adequate teaching materials.

All too soon it was time for us to leave Thamanya. The *Hsayadaw* came halfway with us along the road leading out of his domain. Before he turned back we queued up beside his car to take our leave and he blessed each of us individually.

There was much for us to think about as we drove away toward Pa-an. (We were no longer in the Pajero: it had been sent ahead with the heaviest members of our party in it in the hope that their combined weight would help to keep it from plunging about too wildly.) The mere contrast between the miles of carelessly constructed and ill-maintained roads we had travelled from Rangoon and the smoothness of the roads in Thamanya had shown us that no project could be successfully implemented without the willing co-operation of those concerned. People will contribute hard work and money cheerfully if they are handled with kindness and care and if they are convinced that their contributions will truly benefit the public. The works of the *Hsayadaw* are upheld by the donations of devotees who know beyond the shadow of a doubt that everything that is given to him will be used for the good of others. How fine it would be if such a spirit of service were to spread across the land.

Some have questioned the appropriateness of talking about such matters as *metta* (loving-kindness) and *thissa* (truth) in the political context. But politics is about people and what we had seen in Thamanya proved that love and truth can move people more strongly than any form of coercion.

5. The Peacock and the Dragon

The tenth day of the waning moon of the month of Tazaungdine marks National Day in Burma. It is the anniversary of the boycott against the 1920 Rangoon University Act which was seen by the Burmese as a move to restrict higher education to a privileged few. This boycott, which was initiated by university students, gained widespread support and could be said to have been the first step in the movement for an independent Burma. National Day is thus a symbol of the intimate and indissoluble link between political and intellectual freedom and of the vital role that students have played in the politics of Burma.

This year the seventy-fifth anniversary of National Day fell on 16 November. A committee headed by elder politicians and prominent men of letters was formed to plan the commemoration ceremony. It was decided that the celebrations should be on a modest scale in keeping with our financial resources and the economic situation of the country. The programme was very simple: some speeches, the presentation of prizes to those who had taken part in essay competitions organized by the National League for Democracy, and the playing of songs dating back to the days of the independence struggle. There was also a small exhibition of photographs, old books and magazines.

An unseasonable rain had been falling for several days before the sixteenth but on the morning of National Day itself the weather turned out to be fine and dry. Many of the guests came clad in *pinni*, a hand-woven cotton cloth that ranges in colour from a flaxen beige through varying shades of apricot and orange to burnt umber. During the independence struggle *pinni* had acquired the same significance

19

in Burma as *khaddi* in India, a symbol of patriotism and a practical sign of support for native goods.

Since 1988 it has also become the symbol of the movement for democracy. A *pinni* jacket worn with a white collarless shirt and a Kachin sarong (a tartan pattern in purple, black and green) is the unofficial uniform for 'democracy men'. The dress for 'democracy women' is a *pinni aingyi* (Burmese style blouse) with a traditional hand-woven sarong. During my campaign trip to the state of Kachin in 1989 I once drove through an area considered unsafe because it was within a zone where insurgents were known to be active. For mile upon mile men clad in *pinni* jackets on which the red badge of the NLD gleamed bravely stood as a 'guard of honour' along the route, entirely unarmed. It was a proud and joyous sight.

The seventy-fifth anniversary of National Day brought a proud and joyous sight too. The guests were not all clad in *pinni* but there was about them a brightness that was pleasing to both the eye and the heart. The younger people were full of quiet enthusiasm and the older ones seemed rejuvenated. A well-known student politician of the 1930s who had become notorious in his mature years for the shapeless shirt, shabby denim trousers, scuffed shoes (gum boots during the monsoons) and battered hat in which he would tramp around town was suddenly transformed into a dapper gentleman in full Burmese national costume. All who knew him were stunned by the sudden picture of elegance he presented and our photographer hastened to record such an extraordinary vision.

The large bamboo and thatch pavilion that had been put up to receive the thousand guests was decorated with white banners on which were printed the green figure of a dancing peacock. As a backdrop to the stage there was a large dancing peacock, delicately executed on a white disc. This bird is the symbol of the students who first awoke the political consciousness of the people of Burma. It represents a national movement that culminated triumphantly with the independence of the country.

The orchestra had arrived a little late as there had been an attempt to try to 'persuade' the musicians not to perform at our celebration. But their spirits were not dampened. They stayed on after the end of the official ceremony to play and sing nationalist songs from the old days. The most popular of these was *Nagani*, 'Red Dragon'. *Nagani* was the name of a book club founded by a group of young politicians in 1937 with the intention of making works on politics, economics, history and literature accessible to the people of Burma. The name of the club became closely identified with patriotism and a song was written about the prosperity that would come to the country through the power of the Red Dragon.

Nagani was sung by a young man with a strong, beautiful voice and we all joined in the chorus while some of the guests went up on stage and performed Burmese dances. But beneath the light-hearted merriment ran a current of serious intent. The work of our national movement remains unfinished. We have still to achieve the prosperity promised by the dragon. It is not yet time for the triumphant dance of the peacock.

6. Young Birds Outside Cages

There is a well-known book by Ludu U Hla, one of the foremost literary figures of modern Burma, about the heart-rending fate of young prisoners. The title of this book translates literally as *Caged Young Birds* or *Young Birds Inside Cages*. During the last seven years many young people have been put into the prisons of Burma for their part in the democracy movement. But it is not about them that I would like to write today, it is about the other young people, those who are left outside when one, or in a few cases, both of their parents are imprisoned for their political beliefs.

Throughout the years of my house arrest my family was living in a free society and I could rest assured that they were economically secure and safe from any kind of persecution. The vast majority of my colleagues who were imprisoned did not have the comfort of such an assurance. They knew well that their families were in an extremely vulnerable position, in constant danger of interrogation, house searches, general harassment and interference with their means of livelihood. For those prisoners with young children it was particularly difficult.

In Burma those who are held to endanger state security can be arrested under a section of the law that allows detention for a maximum period of three years. And prisoners who have not been tried are not entitled to visits from their families. A number of political prisoners who were put in jail for their part in the democracy movement were kept there without trial for more than two years. For this time, they did not see their families at all. Only after they were tried and sentenced were they allowed family visits: these visits, permitted once a fortnight, lasted for a mere fifteen minutes.

Two years is a long time in the life of a child. It is long enough for a baby to forget a parent who has vanished from sight. It is long enough for boys and girls to grow up into young adolescents. It is long enough to turn a carefree youngster into a troubled human being. Fifteen minutes once a fortnight is not enough to reverse the effects on a child of the sudden absence of one of the two people to whom it has habitually looked for protection and guidance. Nor is it enough to bridge the gap created by a long separation.

A political prisoner failed to recognize the teenager who came to see him on his first family visit after more than two years in detention as the young son he had left behind. It was a situation that was familiar to me. When I saw my younger son again for the first time after a separation of two years and seven months he had changed from a round faced not-quite-twelve-year-old into a rather stylish 'cool' teenager. If I had met him in the street I would not have known him for my little son.

Political prisoners have to speak to their families through a double barrier of iron grating and wire netting so that no physical contact is possible. The children of one political prisoner would make small holes in the netting and push their fingers through to touch their father. When the holes got visibly large the jail authorities had them patched up with thin sheets of tin. The children would start all over again trying to bore a hole through to their father: it is not the kind of activity one would wish for any child.

I was not the only woman political detainee in Burma: there have been – and there still remain – a number of other women imprisoned for their political beliefs. Some of these women had young children who suddenly found themselves in the care of fathers worried sick for their wives and totally unused to running a household. Most of the children, except for those who were too young to understand what was going on, suffered from varying degrees of stress.

Some children who went to élitist schools found that their school-mates avoided them and that even teachers treated them with a certain reserve: it did not do to demonstrate sympathy for the offspring of a political prisoner and it was considered particularly shocking when the prisoner was a woman. Some children were never taken on visits to prison as it was thought the experience would be too traumatic for them, so for years they were totally deprived of all contact with their mothers. Some children who needed to be reassured that their mothers still existed would be taken on a visit to the prison only to be deeply disturbed by the sight of their mothers looking wan and strange in their white jail garb.

When the parents are released from prison it is still not the end of the story. The children suffer from a gnawing anxiety that their fathers or mothers might once again be taken away and placed out of their reach behind barriers of brick and iron. They have known what it is like to be young birds fluttering helplessly outside the cages that shut their parents away from them. They know that there will be no security for their families as long as freedom of thought and freedom of political action are not guaranteed by the law of the land.

7. Breakfast Blues

One of the most popular topics of conversation in Burma today is the rampant inflation. When a group of people gather together to discuss the situation of the country the talk invariably turns into a comparison of the present prices of goods with the prices that prevailed before 1990. The comparisons are made wistfully, indignantly, incredulously, furiously. It is a subject that never fails to interest everyone, except for the tiny handful of the extremely rich who do not have to worry about the price of anything.

Inflation is the worst enemy of the housewives who have to make a limited income stretch to cover the basic everyday needs of the family. A visit to the bazaar becomes an obstacle race where the shopper has to negotiate carefully between brick walls of impossible prices and pitfalls of sub-standard goods. After an exhausting session of shopping, the housewife goes back home and struggles to produce meals which her family can enjoy, trying to think up substitutes for the more expensive ingredients which she has been forced to strike off her shopping list.

To understand the difficulties of housekeeping, let us look at what it involves to produce just the first meal of the day. Breakfast for many people in Burma is fried rice. Usually it is a mixture of cooked rice and other leftovers from the evening before, vegetables, meat or shrimps; sometimes an egg or two is stirred into it; sometimes there might be a sprinkling of thinly sliced Chinese pork sausage; sometimes a variety of steamed beans sold by vendors in the early hours of the morning might be added. It is a fairly substantial and tasty meal.

But the breakfast fried rice has now taken on an anaemic hue for many families. There is not likely to be any meat or shrimps left over from supper, eggs or Chinese sausage would be an extravagance and even steamed beans, once the humble man's food, are no longer cheap.

The price of chicken six years ago was 100 kyats a viss (about 1.6 kilograms), now it is 400 kyats. Mutton that cost 150 kyats a viss is also 400 kyats now. Pork has gone up from 70 kyats a viss to 280 kyats. The smallest shrimps which cost about 40 kyats a viss in the late 1980s now cost over 100 kyats, while the price of medium-size prawns has gone up from about 100 kyats a viss to over 200. And giant prawns now at over 1000 kyats a viss have entirely disappeared from the tables of all except the very wealthy.

At such prices, few families are able to cook sufficient meat to satisfy the whole family for one meal, let alone to have enough left over for the breakfast fried rice. Eggs are not a ready substitute either as the price of an egg has also leapt up, from about 1 kyat each before to 6 kyats at present. And the Chinese sausages which can be so conveniently sliced up and thrown in to provide flavour and sustenance have become almost a luxury item at around 450 kyats a viss. (Before 1990 the cost was about 250 kyats a viss.)

With the price of meat so high, in the breakfast fried rice of Burma today vegetables feature large – but not as large as one might expect. The price of vegetables has gone up at an even faster rate than the price of meat.

A dish which is much loved by the Burmese not only at breakfast time but at any time of the day is *mohinga*. This is a peppery fish broth, which some have eulogistically termed Burmese bouillabaisse, eaten with rice vermicelli. A steaming bowl of *mohinga* adorned with vegetable fritters, slices of fish cake and hard-boiled eggs and enhanced with the flavour of chopped coriander leaves, morsels of crispy fried garlic, fish sauce, a squeeze of lime and chillies is a wonderful way of stoking up for the day ahead.

The price of an average dish of *mohinga* which includes vegetable fritters and a quarter of a duck egg was 3 kyats before 1990. Now a slightly smaller portion with a cheap bean fritter and without duck egg costs 15 kyats. There is less of even the standard flavourings; coriander leaves have gone up in price from 50 pyas a bunch to 5 kyats. Extras such as fish cake or eggs are, it need hardly be said, expensive. Few people can afford a substantial breakfast of *mohinga*.

These days whether breakfast is fried rice or *mohinga*, it is not only less appetizing from lack of good ingredients, it is also less nourishing. And this is not merely because the high prices of meat, fish and beans mean less protein foods. In both fried rice and *mohinga*, palm oil is used instead of peanut oil which has become too expensive. To make up for the lack of tasty ingredients, a liberal dose of monosodium glutamate is generally added. What used to be a healthy, substantial, delicious breakfast has become for many Burmese not just unsatisfactory but also something of a health hazard.

Yet those who can afford to have fried rice or *mohinga* for breakfast, however unsatisfactory it may be, are the fortunate ones. There are many who have to make do with rice gruel – or even with nothing at all.

8. Christmas in Rangoon

Burmese people love festivals. There is something to celebrate every month of the year. There are the better known festivals such as *Thingyan* (the water festival) in April and *Thidingyut* (the light festival) in October as well as lesser known ones such as those connected with the religious examinations held for monks. In spite of the large number of our own festivals we are not averse to celebrating those of other countries and cultures. Whether it is the Muslim *Id*, the Hindu *Divali*, the Chinese New Year or Christmas, the Burmese are quite ready to take part in the fun and feasting.

When I was a child there used to be Christmas fairs in aid of various charities where Santa Claus, sweltering in his full regalia of thick red robes and flowing white cotton-wool beard, would be in charge of the Lucky Dip counter. At one of those fairs I won a bottle of whisky, which was then a rare and expensive object. Of course to me it was a total disappointment, as I had been hoping for a toy or at least a packet of sweets, and I was thoroughly puzzled by the number of old men (at least they seemed old to me then) who congregated to congratulate me on my great good fortune. My mother advised me to give away the bottle to one of the enthusiastic throng around me, which I did willingly, but I could not understand why the recipient was so effusive in his thanks. The whole incident somewhat diminished my faith both in lucky dips and in adult taste.

Christmas in Rangoon is not yet quite the commercial festival it has become in many of the larger cities of Asia. But there is an increasing selection of Christmas decorations, all made in Asian countries, and of Christmas cakes on sale during the season. Christmas is seen as a time for eating together and exchanging gifts in an atmosphere of mutual goodwill, whether or not one belongs to the Christian faith.

Carol-singing is an activity which instantly recalls pictures of rosy-cheeked children and hearty adults, all wrapped in thick coats with colourful scarves wound around their necks, standing under a Victorian lamp amidst a gentle swirl of snowflakes. Thick coats, woolly scarves, Victorian lamps and snowflakes are not part of any Christmas scene in Rangoon, but here too we have carol singers, usually groups collecting for charity.

A carol-singing group which has been coming to our house every Christmas for many years, since my mother was alive, is from a Christian institution for the blind. Last week they came again, after a gap of six years. The blind singers and guitarist were led by three or four sighted persons as they made their rounds, part of the way on foot and part of the way on public buses. By the time they reached our house it was late in the afternoon, but their voices were still strong and fresh as they sang of peace and joy and goodwill among men. Later as we talked over coffee and sesame crisps, I learnt that the sighted members were themselves children of blind parents and that there were in the institution several blind couples with young children, none of whom suffered from any visual defects. It sounded as though the inmates were one large family, no doubt with the usual quota of family difficulties but quietly determined to lead a full, independent life.

The next day came another group of carol singers from an international organization. They too were collecting for charity and among them were many non-Christians. The day had been warm and there were a large number of outsized mosquitoes swooping and attacking with the swift aggression of dive-bombers. The song of 'Rudolf the Red-Nosed Reindeer' in cold, snowy Santa Claus country sounded a little surreal under the circumstances, but this did not detract from the seasonal cheer.

Because they knew my sons were coming, friends had comman-deered from other friends a potted plant (perhaps a species of Chamaecyparis?) that approximated to a Christmas tree 'for the children' and decorated it with lights and baubles. We produced presents to pile at the foot of the tree and on Christmas Day itself gave lunch to all our regular helpers, numbering about a hundred. After giving out the presents, we had a Lucky Dip. Remembering the time when I had been so disappointed by the bottle of whisky, I had chosen prizes which were entirely different. The best one was an 'executive stress tester' which proved immensely popular. Of all those who tried it out to see who had nerves of steel we discovered that two young men who came from a part of Rangoon known for its strong political traditions did best. They were careful and steady and had tremendous powers of concentration. Such are obviously the qualities necessary for those who wish to pursue politics in Burma. Let us hope the New Year will bring the right atmosphere of goodwill in which these qualities will be allowed to flower.

9. New Year Notes

Our family saw in the beginning of 1986 with Japanese friends in a small town in the vicinity of Kyoto, in fact on a hillside overlooking Lake Biwa. The last evening of 1985 was clear and mild and we all walked leisurely down to a local temple discussing, among other innocuous subjects, the beauty of fireflies. At the temple we waited until midnight, then joined in the ringing of the *joya no o kane* (the bells ringing in the New Year). The sound of the bells floating out through the velvety night seemed to me an assurance that the coming year would be an exceptionally happy one. And indeed 1986 was a most pleasant year, even though it began with a slight domestic upset in our friends' household.

Noriko, our hostess, had asked her husband, Sadayoshi, to take charge of the *o-mochi* (rice cakes) baking in the oven. Sadayoshi, a typical academic who found it difficult to give to anything so mundane as cooking the meticulous attention he brought to his research, failed to check regularly on the *o-mochi*, with the result that the beautiful rice dumplings were slightly charred. Now, Noriko is an excellent cook who accepts nothing short of perfection in her kitchen. Once, shopping with her in Oxford, I had been awed by her majestic demeanour at the butcher's. She asked for veal and the butcher asked which cut she required. 'The best,' she replied serenely. Then she asked for steak, and when the butcher enquired what kind of steak she would like, she again answered, 'The best.' And so it went on. For one such as Noriko, the charred *o-mochi* was a disaster. To prove to Noriko that the slight charring had done nothing to detract from the essentially comforting texture and flavour of the *o-mochi*, I ate five. I like to think that this act of stamina stood me in good stead throughout 1986, which was a year of much travelling.

Now, ten years on, my family and I saw out 1995 in a way that was somewhat remote from Lake Biwa, *joya no o kane* and *o-mochi*. In Rangoon one does not hear the pealing of bells at midnight on 31 December. It was merely the tooting of car horns which told us that 1995 was over and 1996 had begun. The Burmese in general do not celebrate the beginning of the year according to the Gregorian calendar, since the New Year according to our Lunar calendar takes place only in April. Yet here too, as elsewhere throughout the world, January is a time for renewal and hope, for resolutions and rededications.

Perhaps the hopes that fill the hearts of the people of Burma are not quite the same as those with which the people of Japan look forward to 1996. For how many people in Japan would a reasonable price of rice form the core of their hopes for a happier New Year? The days are long past when a variation in the price of rice meant the difference between sufficiency and malnutrition to the ordinary Japanese. Yet there must be many in Japan who remember what it was like when the country was still a largely agricultural economy striving to rise above the terrible devastation brought about by the war.

A professor of geography in Kyoto explained to me in poetic terms his emotions as a child growing up in Japan at the end of the war. He described a day when an American soldier had appeared at his village in search of antiques. He had looked up at the tall stranger and was filled with a strong awareness that he, the little Japanese boy, was ill-nourished, puny and ill-clothed, while the big American soldier was well-dressed and obviously well-fed. He recognized the world of difference between the strong and the weak. But, the professor told me, all through his childhood, as he and his family struggled for daily survival, he would always look up toward the heavens and know that behind the clouds was the sun.

When he was a grown man and Japan had become an economically powerful country, he went on a field trip to an Indian village. And one day as he stood speaking to some Indian villagers he suddenly became aware that he was well-fed and well-clothed while the villagers were malnourished and poorly clothed. He and his countrymen were now cast in the role of the strong. But, as he said to me with a smile, our young people these days, although they are rich and have never known what it is like not to have enough to eat, do not look up toward the heavens, nor do they care whether there are clouds or whether there is a sun behind them.

I do not know how many Japanese people would share the views of this gentle professor of geography. But I think many people in Burma will recognize the instinct that makes us look up toward the heavens and the confident inner voice that tells us that behind the deeply banked clouds there is still the sun waiting to shed its light and warmth at the given hour.

The beginning of a new year is a time when we all like to turn our faces toward the heavens, when we look to our friends all over the world to join us in our quest for light and warmth.

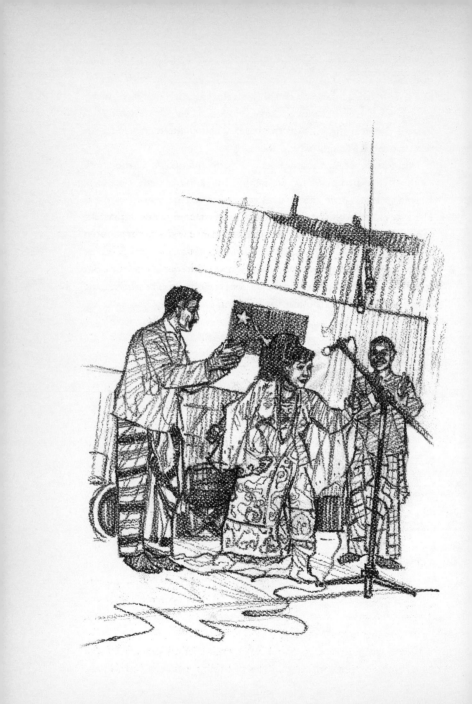

10. An Independent Performance

The *a-nyeint* is a uniquely Burmese form of entertainment consisting of a medley of orchestral music, song and dance and – perhaps most important of all – witty repartee and humorous skits provided by comedians. Traditionally an *a-nyeint* troupe is hired to perform both at family celebrations such as the Buddhist ordination ceremony for boys or on public occasions such as pagoda festivals or jubilees.

The fourth of January this year was the forty-eighth anniversary of the day when Burma became an independent nation. The NLD made plans to include in its programme to commemorate Independence Day a performance of *a-nyeint* by a troupe from Mandalay. During the week before Independence Day, members of the youth wing of the NLD had been rehearsing another item on the programme, a short one-act play that concluded with a song about freedom. Perhaps it was the resounding refrain of this song, repeated again and again, that made the authorities view the forthcoming NLD celebrations with a jaundiced eye. It was conveyed to us that our entertainment programme should not include either *dobat* or a play. A *dobat* is a double-sided Burmese drum, to the rousing rhythm of which are sung songs in the folk tradition, often very witty, with a satirical content that is not always pleasing to the powers that be. We had not in fact planned any *dobat* songs and there seemed no good reason for cancelling the play, whose principal theme simply underlined the importance of unity and the need to solve political problems through dialogue. It was therefore decided that the programme would be carried through as planned.

On the evening of 2 January a key member of my office staff was pulled in by his local military intelligence unit for twenty-four hours.

He was interrogated not only on such crucial matters as the policies and decision-making process of our party but also on our proposed Independence Day ceremony. The authorities did not seem particularly keen on the idea of our commemorating the occasion in a spirit of freedom. However, the *a-nyeint* was not mentioned.

At eight o'clock in the morning on 4 January there was a commemoration ceremony in the grounds of a small rope factory organized by members of the *Dohbama Asi-ayone*, the political organization that had been at the core of the struggle to liberate Burma from colonial rule. The hoary veterans conducted the proceedings with all the élan and verve possible under the restricted circumstances, their ageing voices strengthened by their convictions as they repeated their dedication to the cause of freedom and national unity.

The Independence Day ceremony of the NLD began late in the morning in the garden of my house and was expected to be completed within three hours. In the event the programme went on for six hours because the audience of nearly 2000 wanted the last item, the *a-nyeint*, to continue for as long as possible.

It started in the traditional way with two comedians coming forward to introduce the performance. But as soon as the senior of the two, U Pa Pa Lay, started to speak it became obvious, to the surprise and untold delight of the audience, that this was going to be an act such as had not been witnessed in Burma for several decades. The comedians were determined to exercise to the full their traditional right to apply their comic and critical powers to a commentary on matters of topical interest, many of a political nature.

U Pa Pa Lay began by saying that this was an occasion when he would be acting and speaking according to his own wishes and that he was aware such audacity would very likely land him in prison. He explained that he had already served a year in prison for making a joke that referred to the overwhelming support for the NLD throughout the whole country. The thunderous applause that greeted U Pa Pa Lay's introductory remarks was a fitting prelude to a performance that scintillated with witty skits, brilliant jokes, sprightly dances and lively music. The audience revelled in the artistic skill of the whole performance and were filled with deep admiration for the courage of the company, in particular for U Pa Pa Lay and his fellow comedian U Lu Zaw who so bravely gave voice to what the people had been wishing – but not daring – to say for many a year.

On the afternoon of 6 January the troupe came to say goodbye to me before they went back to Mandalay. They knew that they were very likely to be arrested soon but they were extremely cheerful. They assured me nothing would detract from the great satisfaction achieved from a performance conducted entirely in accordance with their own wishes. The company arrived back in Mandalay on the morning of the seventh and later that day they were all taken away by the authorities. We are now waiting for the next act in the drama of this most courageous troupe. Come what may, we shall stand by them.

11. A Note on Economic Policy

Interviews with members of the media have become part of my normal work schedule over the last seven months. Some interviews are brief, fifteen minutes or so limited to a particular topic which is the speciality of the newspaper or magazine concerned. Other interviews are longer and ramble over a wider range of subjects. There are a number of standard questions related to the period of my house arrest and the work of the NLD which are asked in almost every interview. Then there are questions which relate to current developments.

In recent weeks many journalists have asked about the economic policies of the NLD. One or two have even asked if we believed in an open-market economy. It brought home to me the fact that few foreigners knew of the existence of the Manifesto brought out by our party for the 1990 elections. As there has been no official English translation of the Manifesto, even those who knew of it might not have known much about its contents. (The authorities have not permitted the NLD to bring out any publications since about two months after the elections.)

In view of the current media interest, I would like to list here the economic objectives of the NLD as stated under eleven clauses in the section of the Manifesto on the economy:

a) Stability in prices, currency and employment; a national currency in which people can have confidence

b) Appropriate monetary and fiscal policies and an effectively controlled budget

c) A review of the exchange rate followed by necessary revision

d) Priority given to the import of fuel, vehicles and other goods that will contribute towards a fall in prices

e) Diversification of export goods

f) Amendments to foreign investment laws with a view to increasing the volume of investments

g) Reduction of foreign debts and resumption of aid and assistance from abroad

h) Review and, where necessary, revision or repeal of laws, decrees, regulations and other restrictions that circumscribe economic activities

i) Review and revision of the tax system to make private enterprise more profitable

j) An economy in which all the component parts are based fully on the market economy; encouragement of the speedy development of private enterprise

k) Promotion of a more efficient tourist industry.

Of course it is easy enough to set down economic objectives, the question is how one sets about achieving them. I have found the opinions expressed by Dr David Dapice, Associate Faculty Fellow of the Harvard Institute for International Development, in his reports on the Burmese economy to the United Nations Development Programme very similar to the views of the NLD. In 'Prospects for Sustainable Growth in Myanmar/Burma' Dr Dapice comments that 'Economic reform is not simply setting an interest rate or an exchange rate. It is establishing a shared vision of where the policies should lead and creating credibility and confidence that most movements will be in the right direction.'[1]

Credibility and confidence are basic to good business, and are what we must first establish if we want our policies to lead to a successful open-market economy. It is for this reason that the NLD believes that essential to sound economic development is a political system firmly rooted in the rule of law. Here again, I would like to refer to Dr Dapice who holds that to reverse the trend in Burma towards 'serious and difficult-to-reverse economic, social and political problems' there would need to be 'a strong and effective legal system, and a set of policies and institutions that engender confidence enough for people to save in banks and invest in the future without fear that they will, effectively, lose even if they succeed.'[2]

44

When I am questioned as to my views on foreign investment I reply that now is not yet the time to invest. And to those who would query what the alternative to 'investment now' would be, I would say: 'invest in the future'. That is to say, invest in democracy for Burma if only for the sake of your own profits. Businesses that frame their investment policies with a view to promoting an open, secure political system based on confidence and credibility will find they are also promoting an open, secure economy based on confidence and credibility where optimum returns can be expected by investors. A democratic Burma will be an economically dynamic and stable Burma.

1 David Dapice, 'Prospects for Sustainable Growth in Myanmar/Burma' [A Report to the United Nations Development Programme, 12 September 1995], p. 15.
2 *Ibid.*

12. Months and Seasons

It is generally held that in Burma we do not have four seasons, we have only three, the hot season, the rainy season and the cold season. Spring is largely unknown although in the cooler border regions there is a stretch of pleasant, spring-like weather that we refer to as early summer. Neither is there a season that the Japanese would easily recognize as autumn, but in those parts of the country where there are deciduous trees a flush of *momiji* (Japanese maple tree) colours brighten the early weeks of the cold season.

From a casual observation of Burmese behaviour it might appear as though we were not particularly sensitive to the changing seasons. We do not have festivals to celebrate the advent of spring blossoms, we do not acknowledge the vibrant beauty of the autumn, we do not incorporate seasonal motifs into our artistic presentations or our fashions. We wear the same kind of clothes the whole year round: the main sartorial difference between the hot season and the rainy season is an umbrella and in the cold season we simply add a few more layers to our summer outfits. We do not give the impression of paying much attention to seasonal variations.

But the Burmese are in fact acutely aware of the minute changes that take place in their natural surroundings throughout the year. In the classical tradition we recognize six seasons and we also have a genre of poetry that treats the twelve months of our lunar calendar as though each month were a separate season in itself.

December coincides roughly with the month of *Natdaw* which, in the days before Buddhism took root in Burma, was a time for the worship of the Hindu god Ganesh, the elephant-headed deity of wealth. In poetic tradition, *Natdaw* is the month when the earth is wrapped in mists and cold silvery dews and hearts are filled with longing for absent loved ones. It is the month when the *thazin* orchid blooms: tiny exquisite blossoms, parchment-coloured with golden yellow stamens, drooping from a curve of translucent green stems. For the Burmese the *thazin* is exceedingly romantic, delicate and difficult to nurture, its graceful beauty barely separable from the sharp coolness of the season when it comes into flower.

Natdaw constitutes the second half of the season of *Hemanta* or winter. It is the most lovely, most nostalgic of seasons in Burma. The skies are porcelain-bright, pale-cerulean edged with duck-egg blue at the horizon. In Rangoon the coldest day is no colder than a fine day in Kyoto at the time of the cherry blossom. But for the Burmese this is cold indeed.

Elderly gentlemen cover their heads in woollen balaclavas when they go out for their early morning constitutional and old ladies drape knitted shawls over flannel or velvet jackets of a cut fashionable half a century ago. Tradition recommends the consumption of rich and warming foods such as meat, milk, butter, honey and dried ginger during *Hemanta* and the cheeks of those who can afford to eat well become rounded and glow in the fresh morning air.

Winter begins for me when at night I start piling on the Chin blankets that we have always used in our family. These blankets of thick cotton come in stripes or checks, usually in different shades of greens, reds and reddish browns. As children we become attached to our own blankets and I remember in particular a green checked one that I insisted on using until it was almost in tatters. Now, the first blanket I place on my bed at the advent of the cold weather is an old one given to my father by Chin friends: it is white with faded red stripes and in the corner is the date embroidered by my mother, '25–3–47'. When the temperature drops further I place on top of the Chin blanket a Japanese one that formed part of my parents' bridal bed.

This is the eighth winter that I have not been able to get into bed at night without thinking of prisoners of conscience and other inmates of jails all over Burma. As I lie on a good mattress under a mosquito net, warm in my cocoon of blankets, I cannot help but remember that many of my political colleagues are lying in bleak cells on thin mats through which seeps the peculiarly unpleasant chill of a concrete floor. Both their clothing and their blankets will be quite inadequate and they are unprotected by mosquito nets. There are not as many mosquitoes in the winter as there are in summer but a net would have provided some much needed extra warmth. I wonder how many prisoners lie awake shivering through the night, how many of the older ones suffer from aching bones and cramped muscles, how many are dreaming of a hot drink and other comforts of home.

This is the eighth winter that I have got out of bed in the morning and looked out at the clean freshness of the world and wondered how many prisoners are able to savour the beauties of *Hemanta* of which our poets have written so nostalgically. It would be interesting to read poems of winter behind the unyielding walls of prisons which shut out silvery dew and gossamer sunshine, the smell of pale winter blossoms and the taste of rich warming foods.

13. Visiting Rites

The Burmese are reputed to be one of the most hospitable people in the world. When I was a child I took it for granted that formal invitations to lunch or tea or dinner were issued only to foreigners. Burmese friends simply dropped in and shared whatever you happened to be eating. And there was always enough for visitors, however unexpected. Often friends would suddenly appear in the evening, hot green tea, palm candy, fried beans and *laphet* (preserved tea leaves) would be brought out and there would be an impromptu party. Sometimes the conversation flowed so happily and the atmosphere was so congenial the visitors would decide to stay for the night. That would be no problem at all: some smooth *thinbyu* mats of the finest quality, pillows, blankets and mosquito nets and any room with a fresh breeze blowing through would be instantly transformed into a pleasant guest dormitory. Night would descend on a household replete with food and the sense of hospitality well discharged.

There is no tradition of inns or hotels in Burma. Visitors from out of town stay with friends or relatives for as long as it is necessary. Considerate guests come laden with food and other gifts and everybody enjoys the opportunity to exchange news of births, deaths, marriages, mild scandals and success stories. Sometimes guests stay on so long that their hosts become a little restive. But there are also guests so cherished that their visit is extended day after day at the behest of the hosts. Having guests to stay is an informal and elastic process.

Hospitality is no longer so simple. Apart from the high food prices that make most people hesitate to impose themselves on friends, staying overnight in a house other than your own involves more than friendship, good conversation and a cool mat. Visitors must make up their minds before too late an hour if they intend to stay the night because their presence has to be reported to the local Law and Order Restoration Council (LORC) before nine o'clock in the evening. Failure to 'report the guest list' could result in a fine or a prison sentence for both the guest and the host. Nobody may go away for the night from his own home without informing the local LORC as well as the LORC of the place where he will be staying. The authorities have the right to check at any time during the night to see if there are any unreported guests or if any of the members of the family are missing. Households which shelter members of the NLD or their supporters tend to be subjected to frequent 'guest checks' these days.

These periodic checks can be a mere formality conducted with courtesy or they can be a form of harassment. There is no lack of cases where the authorities have marched in at the dead of night and flung up mosquito nets to ascertain that the sleeping population tallied with the names and numbers on Form 10. Form 10 is the list of all the members of a family. In some households which comprise more than one nuclear family there may be more than one Form 10. Domestic employees who sleep at their employers' homes also have to be registered on Form 10 or they have to be reported as guests. A person may be registered on only one Form 10, so if it is necessary for him to be entered as a member of another family for some reason, his name has to be removed from the original family list.

During the days of the Burma Socialist Programme Party (BSPP), Form 10 played a central role in the daily lives of the people of Burma. In accordance with the household members listed on the form, it was decided how much a family was entitled to buy of such essentials as rice, oil, salt, chillies, onions, soap and milk powder from the government co-operative. Today the co-operatives no longer supply consumer necessities, so Form 10 has ceased to be important in the economic life of the average family. However, it still features large in the family's social life because it decides who may or may not spend the night in a house without reporting to the authorities.

And what can happen if a family fails to let the local LORC know they have an overnight guest? Both the guest and the host are liable to a minimum fine of 50 kyats, or to a prison sentence ranging from two weeks to six months. Since 1988, the cases of prison sentences meted out to unreported guests have increased hugely. Some of the cases are tragicomic. A young man caught spending the night as an unreported guest was taken to court together with his host. The court handed down a prison sentence of six months to the guest and two weeks to the host. The host, a hospitable man with a long experience of paying fines for his unexpected and unreported guests, involuntarily clicked his tongue against his teeth in astonished disgust. The acting magistrate heard the loud click and promptly changed the sentence on the host to one month's imprisonment for contempt of court. The price of hospitality in Burma can be very high.

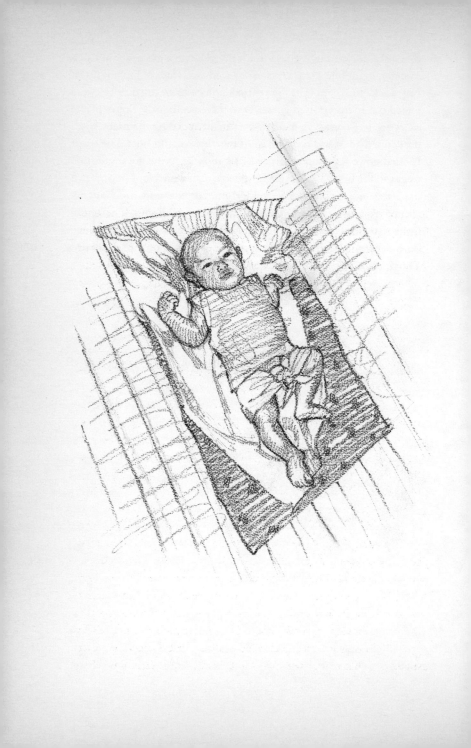

14. A Baby in the Family

A couple of weeks ago some friends of mine became grandparents for the first time when their daughter gave birth to a little girl. The husband accepted his new status as grandfather with customary joviality, while the wife, too young-looking and pretty to get into the conventional idea of a cosily aged grandmother, found it a somewhat startling experience. The baby was the first grandchild for the 'boy's side' as well, so she was truly a novel addition to the family circle, the subject of much adoring attention. I was told the paternal grandfather was especially pleased because the baby had been born in the Burmese month of *Pyatho* – an auspicious time for the birth of a girl child.

In societies where the birth of a girl is considered a disaster, the atmosphere of excitement and pride surrounding my friends' granddaughter would have caused astonishment. In Burma there is no prejudice against girl babies. In fact, there is a general belief that daughters are more dutiful and loving than sons and many Burmese parents welcome the birth of a daughter as an assurance that they will have somebody to take care of them in their old age.

My friends' granddaughter was only twelve days old when I went to admire her. She lay swaddled in pristine white on a comfortable pile of blankets and sheets spread on the wooden floor of my friends' bungalow, a small dome of mosquito netting arched prettily over her. It had been a long time since I had seen such a tiny baby and I was struck by its miniature perfection. I do not subscribe to the Wodehousian view that all babies look like poached eggs. Even if they do not have clearly defined features, babies have distinct expressions that mark them off as individuals from birth. And they certainly have individual cries, a fact I learned soon after the birth of my first son. It took me a few hours to realize that the yells of each tiny vociferous inmate of the maternity hospital had its own unique pitch, cadence, range and grace-notes.

My friends' grandchild, however, did not provide me with a chance to familiarize myself with her particular milk call. Throughout my visit she remained as inanimate and still as a carved papoose on display in a museum, oblivious of the fuss and chatter around her. At one time her eyelids fluttered slightly and she showed signs of stirring but it was a false alarm. She remained resolutely asleep even when I picked her up and we all clustered around to have our photograph taken with the new star in our firmament.

Babies, I have read somewhere, are specially constructed to present an appealingly vulnerable appearance aimed at arousing tender, protective instincts: only then can tough adults be induced to act as willing slaves to demanding little beings utterly incapable of doing anything for themselves. It is claimed that there is something about the natural smell of a baby's skin that invites cuddles and kisses. Certainly I like both the shape and smell of babies, but I wonder whether their attraction does not lie in something more than merely physical attributes. Is it not the thought of a life stretching out like a shining clean slate on which might one day be written the most beautiful prose and poetry of existence that engenders such joy in the hearts of the parents and grandparents of a newly born child? The birth of a baby is an occasion for weaving hopeful dreams about the future.

However, in some families parents are not able to indulge in long dreams over their children. The infant mortality rate in Burma is 94 per 1000 live births, the fourth highest among the nations of the East Asia and Pacific Region. The mortality rate for those under the age of five too is the fourth highest in the region, 147 per 1000. And the maternal mortality rate is the third highest in the region at the official rate of 123 per 100 000 live births. (United Nations agencies surmise that the actual maternal mortality rate is in fact higher, 140 or more per 100 000.)

The reasons for these high mortality rates are malnutrition, lack of access to safe water and sanitation, lack of access to health services and lack of caring capacity, which includes programmes for childhood development, primary education and health education. In summary, there is a strong need in Burma for greater investment in health and education. Yet government expenditure in both sectors, as a proportion of the budget, has been falling steadily. Education accounted for 5.9 per cent of the budget in 1992–3, 5.2 per cent in 1993–4 and 5 per cent in 1994–5. Similarly, government spending on health care has dropped from 2.6 per cent in 1992–3, to 1.8 per cent in 1993–4 and 1.6 per cent in 1994–5.

Some of the best indicators of a country developing along the right lines are healthy mothers giving birth to healthy children who are assured of good care and a sound education that will enable them to face the challenges of a changing world. Our dreams for the future of the children of Burma have to be woven firmly around a commitment to better health care and better education.

15. Days of Rest

People ask me in what way my life has changed since I was released from house arrest eight months ago. One of the most obvious changes is that I can no longer keep to the strict timetable that governed my days when I lived alone. Then, it was important to establish a routine and to follow it strictly to avoid feckless squandering of time. I rose at half past four every morning and turned the light off at nine o'clock at night. I did not have to wonder how many hours of sleep I would be able to grab. To introduce some variety that would divide my days into a pattern that reflected the ebb and flow of ordinary life, I kept Saturday and Sunday significantly different from the rest of the week.

There was always a holiday feeling to the beginning of the weekend. Forty-eight hours of marvellous emptiness stretched before me to be filled with leisurely activity. I still rose at half past four in the morning and started with an hour of meditation, as I did during the week, but once the meditation was over I let the day flow around me without any hurry. I would carry out little chores, such as putting the contents of a cupboard into order or sorting out the sewing box, which gave great satisfaction without exhaustion. And I would re-read favourite books, savouring the passages that I particularly liked. Sunday was especially luxurious because I would boil myself an egg for breakfast. The weekend would pass all too quickly. Nowadays, too, weekends pass all too quickly but these are weekends of a quite different order from the ones I experienced during my years of house arrest. To begin with Saturday is a full working day. Every week my office staff and I discuss the possibility of arranging a lighter programme for the next week and talk wistfully of a relatively free

Saturday. However, we have not yet succeeded in implementing such a programme.

Happily, 'No appointments on Sunday' is a strict rule. Well, at any rate it is a strict rule in theory. It just sometimes happens that something unavoidable crops up on Sunday. But if there are really no appointments, Sunday morning is wonderful. I can linger over my breakfast cup of tea: I can even read while sipping my tea. I can bathe and wash my hair without haste and I can tidy up the mess that has accumulated over the week. I can savour to the full that lovely, leisurely weekend feeling.

The weekend feeling actually ends on Sunday afternoon, because preparations for the public meeting that takes place at my gate at four o'clock begin after lunch. The young men responsible for the public address system start to test the equipment. 'Testing, testing, one, two, three, four . . .' must be one of the most unattractive phrases in the world, especially when repeated in a monotonous tone through a microphone that emits shrill nerve-jarring shrieks.

Although the quiet weekend air dissipates early on Sunday afternoon, the holiday atmosphere continues. Friends and colleagues start arriving and it is very much like a family gathering. Some of the visitors come laden with food. The wife of U Kyi Maung, one of the deputy chairmen of the NLD, generally brings a large supply of steamed glutinous rice with both sweet and savoury accompaniments such as tiny, crisply fried fish and grated fresh coconut. After the public meeting we sit out in the garden in small groups, drinking hot green tea, eating glutinous rice and exchanging news. An outsider witnessing the animation of the conversation and hearing the gales of laughter bursting out intermittently from each group would not guess that most of the people present worked together every day, voluntarily and without pay, under circumstances which were far from easy.

Most Sundays we manage to get through all that we have to do by about seven o'clock in the evening instead of eight o'clock, which is when we normally end our working day during the week. When all the Sunday helpers and visitors have left, the weekend holiday comes to an end for me because there is usually a considerable amount of reading and writing to be completed before Monday morning. By the time I get to bed it feels as though I am already well into the new week and I often recall a line of a song that a very dear family friend would sing out in her magnificent voice at the conclusion of a busy day: 'Rest from your labours, children of toil, night cometh over, rest ye awhile'.

Journalists ask me from time to time whether it is not a great burden to be engaged in the struggle for human rights and democracy in Burma under the restrictions imposed on the movements of political parties, especially those of the NLD. There are two main reasons why I do not find my work a burden in spite of the difficulties involved. First, I have dedicated and honourable (and good-humoured) colleagues whom I can trust and respect, and second, I gather strength from each day satisfactorily accounted for, including the brief days of rest which I would like to think are well-earned.

16. Union Day Dances

On 12 February 1947 an agreement was signed by Chin, Kachin and Shan leaders and by my father as the representative of the Burmese government. This agreement, which came to be known as the Panglong Agreement after the name of the town in the Shan State where it was signed, stated the belief that 'freedom will be more speedily achieved by the Shans, the Kachins and the Chins by their immediate co-operation with the interim Burmese government'. The Panglong Agreement is proof that the Union of Burma is based on the voluntary decision of different ethnic peoples to unite in the building of an independent nation and 12 February is designated Union Day. It is a day for all the peoples of Burma to rededicate themselves to the spirit of mutual trust and respect that made the Panglong Agreement possible.

The NLD commemorated Union Day with a declaration of its policy on the ethnic peoples of Burma followed by a programme of dances. There was also a small bazaar where textiles from different parts of Burma, souvenirs, hot tea, cold drinks, rice noodles with fish soup, bean noodles and Shan tofu salad were sold. The food stalls did very brisk trade and I can personally vouch for the superiority of the tofu, cool and satin smooth on the tongue.

About 5000 people attended our celebration, the maximum number we could accommodate. There were many more who wanted to attend despite the fact that in certain townships the authorities had threatened unpleasant consequences for those who came to the NLD Union Day ceremony. Karen villagers from Hmawbi township were told they should not dance at our ceremony and it was made impossible for them to rent a car on the morning of 12 February. However, they managed to make their way to us by public transport.

The entertainment began with a solo performance by a Mon dancer. Her costume in flaming burnt orange brocade and her golden head-dress surmounted by the legendary *kintha* bird were very striking, and her movements were precise and graceful with the flexible hand gestures characteristic of so many dances in South-East Asia.

A troupe of Pa-o dancers had come from a village in the Mon State. They made an impressive appearance on the stage, the men in black jackets, wide, black trousers and white shirts, their turbans presenting the only touch of colour. The women were also in black, the tunics and jackets with the merest touch of red and black trimming, their turbans very similar to those of the men. One of the girls accompanied the dancing with songs sung in a high sweet soprano. The most exciting parts of the Pa-o performance were the sword dances executed by the men with solemn finesse.

A Shan contingent which had come up from villages south-east of Rangoon performed the final item – sword dances to the rousing music of drums and cymbals. As the tempo of the music built up, punctuated by an occasional beat on a brass gong, the sword play became very swift and intricate and the audience clapped along with the music, carried away by the rhythm and swayed by the prowess of the performers. At one point members of the audience stood up and danced, unable to contain their enthusiasm. Some of the loudest applause was drawn by the dance with two swords, performed with naked, well-honed blades that flashed under the stage lights as the dancer thrusted and parried and swirled in action.

Earlier in the programme there had been another kind of Shan dancing executed by a group of girls dressed in pink. In addition there had been a solo dance by an Arakanese dancer, Karen dancing, Kayah dancing, Kachin dancing, Chin dancing and a traditional Burmese folk-dance that acted out the words of a chant accompanied by lively music.

Each had its own individual attraction. The Chin dance was quite different from the sword dances which fired such enthusiastic response but it was also extremely popular with the audience. The dancers were clad in beautiful woven cloth, the men with traditional Chin blankets draped toga-fashion. They trod a steady measure around the stage in couples, headed by a tall young man with raised right arm holding up a sword while a pretty girl paced by his side, delicately holding on to his left arm. The rhythm of the music as well as the stateliness of the dance were mesmerizing.

The various dances performed illustrated the wide range of ethnic cultures of which Burma can boast. Unity in diversity has to be the principle of those who genuinely wish to build our country into a strong nation that allows a variety of races, languages, beliefs and cultures to flourish in peaceful and happy co-existence. Only a government that tolerates opinions and attitudes different from its own will be able to create an environment where peoples of diverse traditions and aspirations can breathe freely in an atmosphere of mutual understanding and trust.

17. An Eventful Week

This has been a rather exhausting week. 13 February, the day after Union Day, which we had celebrated so vigorously, was my father's birthday as well as Children's Day in Burma. 130 children, ranging from little tots still unsteady on their feet to slender twelve year olds on the verge of teenage self-consciousness, came to our Children's Day celebration, which had been organized by the youth wing of the NLD.

The children's entertainment included a short skit, poetry recitals and three performances of traditional Burmese dancing. The *nabanhsan* dance that depicted a village belle with her hair tied in bunches above her ear (*nabanhsan* refers to this particular hairstyle) enchanted everybody. It was performed by an exquisite six year old with a vividly expressive face and a delicious dimple in one cheek. As she danced and acted out her role of coquettish beauty, two little boys, one standing on either side of her, went through the motions of admiring rural lads. They had handkerchiefs tied around their heads in the accepted style of rakish young manhood and mimed expertly to the words of the song that accompanied their act. The movement of their hands and the motion of their bodies as they parodied flute-playing and finger-whistling drew thunderous applause. One of the little boys had such a look of sweet devilry, mischief sparkling in his eyes, that his face was a whole entertainment in itself. On the basis of the *nabanhsan* dance alone, many in the audience were ready to vote the children more talented than the adults who had performed on Union Day.

The seriousness with which these young children approached their artistic training was impressive while the pure enjoyment, unadulterated by stage fright, with which they went through their paces was thoroughly delightful. We were strengthened by the spirit and success of our Union Day celebrations but our Children's Day event was truly refreshing and we felt appropriately rejuvenated.

The 14 February was the first anniversary of the death of U Nu, the first Prime Minister of independent Burma. His family and political associates had arranged a memorial ceremony at a large monastery in Rangoon. On 13 February, the committee responsible for organizing the ceremony was told by the authorities that no politicians were to be invited. The committee explained that invitations had already been sent out and that as U Nu himself was a politician, many of those who would be attending the ceremony were bound to be politicians. That night the local authorities held a meeting to plan what should be done the next day.

It seemed the politicians whom the authorities were particularly anxious to debar from the ceremony were those who belonged to the NLD. It was ordered that things were to be made unpleasant for us when we arrived for the ceremony. We were to be pelted with tomatoes. A number of those who received the orders were filled with disgust and we were quickly informed of the plan. We decided to attend the ceremony as already arranged and should we come across any tomato-throwers to ask them what – or who – had moved them to such action.

At half past six on the morning of the fourteenth, hundreds of people unknown to the organizers of the memorial ceremony turned up at the monastery. There was parked in the vicinity a Toyota car filled with three crates of tomatoes, which were said to have been bought by a police corporal. It was very likely the uninvited guests were members of the Union Solidarity and Development Association (USDA), a so-called social welfare organization formed under the patronage of SLORC. We were told that it was the secretary of the association's eastern district wing who had ordered the tomato offensive. In the event, nothing happened, perhaps because there were too many *bona fide* guests who were staunch supporters of democracy, or perhaps because those who had been sent to create trouble had no stomach for the task that had been set for them.

We were not able to stay long at U Nu's memorial ceremony

because that same morning the first of a series of NLD educational lectures was scheduled to take place. The speaker was Dr Tha Hla, one of the most eminent academics Burma has produced. He was the rector of Rangoon University and later worked for many years with UNESCO. The scope of his scholarship was such that although he had received his doctorate in geology, he chose to speak about a prince who lived from the late thirteenth to early fourteenth centuries whom he saw as the first ruler of Burma to promote unity between the Shans and the Burmese. The lecture, which was both informative and interesting, was followed by a lively discussion between Dr Tha Hla and U Wun, the foremost poet of our country. What a pleasure it was to listen to well-bred men of outstanding intellect courteously exchanging views. How wonderfully reassuring to know that we had among us minds totally removed from the kind of mentality that moves along the lines of organized hooliganism.

Above: U Aung Shwe
Below: U Lwin

18. A Few Introductions (1)

In writing about the activities of the NLD it will be necessary to mention the names of some of our key personnel from time to time, so I would like to introduce a quartet of retired army officers who are leading members of the executive committee of the party.

The Chairman of the NLD is U Aung Shwe. He joined the Burma Independence Army in 1942, one of the educated young men (he graduated from Rangoon University two years previously) who felt they had a duty to serve the country in any way they could during the war years. After Burma became an independent nation in 1948, he continued to serve in the armed forces and by the end of the 1950s, he had become a brigadier, a rank achieved by few in those days. In 1962, while serving as the Commander of Southern Command, he was asked to retire from the army and sent as Burmese Ambassador to Australia and New Zealand. No official explanation of any kind was given for the transfer at the time. However, as part of the campaign to try to discredit the leaders of the NLD in the eyes of the people, it has been written in government publications of recent years that U Aung Shwe had been allowed to retire from the army because he had displayed partisanship during the elections of 1960. It must therefore be assumed that he was a casualty of an attempt by the armed forces to defend themselves from accusations that they tried to engineer the victory of socialists in the said elections.

Subsequent to his posting in Australia, U Aung Shwe served in Egypt and then in Paris until his retirement from government service in 1975. He settled in Rangoon, where in 1988 public demonstrations erupted that eventually spread across the country. The people of Burma were tired of the authoritarian rule of the Burma Socialist

Programme Party (BSPP) that had turned their country, once seen as the fastest-developing nation in South-East Asia, into one of the poorest in the world.

The predictable reaction to the collapse of the one-party system was the mushrooming of parties at a rate which would be familiar to those who knew Japan in the immediate post-war period. Among the parties that sprang up were the NLD, of which U Aung Shwe was an Executive Committee member, and its close official ally, the Patriotic Old Comrades League formed by retired members of the armed forces, of which he was the Chairman. Although there were over 200 political parties, including the BSPP under its new name of National Unity Party, it soon became evident that it was the NLD which had the support of the vast majority of the people of Burma. Even as the popularity and the organizational capacity of the party rose, persecution of its members and restrictions on its activities increased. In June 1989 U Win Tin, one of the two Secretaries of the NLD, was imprisoned and in July, U Tin U, the Chairman, and I, the General Secretary, were placed under house arrest. In spite of such setbacks, the NLD was victorious in an overwhelming 82 per cent of the constituencies during the elections of May 1990. This led not to a transfer to democratic government as the people expected but to a series of intensive measures aimed at debilitating the party. In September U Kyi Maung, who was in effect the acting Chairman of the NLD, was arrested, leaving U Aung Shwe with the unenviable task of piloting the party through a period of burgeoning difficulties.

The only original member of the Executive Committee who was left after 1990 to help U Aung Shwe in his struggle to keep the NLD intact through the years that threatened its viability as a political party, was U Lwin, the Treasurer. U Lwin had joined the Burma Independence Army as an eighteen-year-old boy at the outbreak of the war. In August 1943 he was among a batch of Burmese cadets chosen to go to Japan for training at the Rikugun Shikan Gakko (army academy). By the time the young Burmese officers had completed their training in April 1945, the anti-fascist resistance movement had started and U Lwin and his fellow graduates of the military academy remained in Hakone until October 1945, making charcoal which they sold to buy food.

U Lwin continued with his career in the army after independence and was sent on training courses to England and West Germany. In 1959 he was sent to Washington as military attaché. On his return from the United States he spent some years as Deputy Commander of Central Command, then Commander of South-Eastern Command before he was asked to come back to Rangoon to become a Deputy Minister. As the military government that assumed power in 1962 took on a civilian garb under the Burma Socialist Programme Party, U Lwin served successively as Minister of Finance, Deputy Prime Minister and a member of the State Council. It was as a member of the State Council that he resigned in 1980.

U Lwin joined the NLD in 1988 and was appointed Treasurer because of his experience in finance and his unquestioned integrity. In 1992, when the NLD was forced to reorganize its Executive Committee, U Lwin took on the post of Secretary, while U Aung Shwe became Chairman.

Above: U Kyi Maung
Below: U Tin U

19. A Few Introductions (2)

Among the group of Burmese cadets with whom U Lwin went to Japan for military training in 1943 was a young man who became a particularly close friend and, later, his brother-in-law: U Kyi Maung. At university, U Kyi Maung had been active in the students' movement for independence. In 1938, he marched at the head of a demonstration holding aloft the flag of the Students' Union. Mounted police sent to stop the demonstration rode into the ranks of the students with batons swinging. U Kyi Maung was one of the first students to be struck down, hit in three places on the head. Another student close behind him, Ko Aung Gyaw, also received on the head a single blow that knocked him down. A few hours later, the young man died from his injuries in the hospital, causing great anger throughout the country and raising the tempo of discontent against the colonial government. 'Boh Aung Gyaw', as the student martyr came to be known, remains an inspiration to students fighting for justice and freedom today.

At the outbreak of the war, U Kyi Maung joined the Burma Independence Army, where he came to know many of the men who would form the core of the armed forces of independent Burma. A staunch believer in the importance of an apolitical, professional army, he was strongly opposed to the military takeover of 1962. It was thus hardly surprising that in 1963, at which time he was serving as the Commander of South-Western Command, he was asked to retire from the armed forces.

During the quarter century that followed his retirement from the army, U Kyi Maung was imprisoned twice, for a total of seven years, on suspicion of opposing the military, later the Burma Socialist Programme Party (BSPP), government. Soon after the outbreak of the democracy movement of 1988, U Kyi Maung was put into prison for the third time, but was released within a month. In September 1988, he became one of the twelve members of the Executive Committee of the NLD.

When U Tin U and I were placed under house arrest in July 1989, the Executive Committee of the NLD decided on collective leadership, but it would not be wrong to say that U Kyi Maung was the man who led the party to its resounding victory in the elections of 1990. After the first few weeks of euphoria, the people of Burma began to suspect that the authorities had no intention of honouring the results of the elections. Their worst fears were confirmed when U Kyi Maung was arrested in September 1990, tried by a military tribunal and sentenced to twenty years' imprisonment. He was, however, released in March 1995.

Another eminent leader of the NLD released on the same day as U Kyi Maung was U Tin U. As Chairman of the NLD, he had been placed under house arrest in July 1989 and in December of the same year tried by a military tribunal and sentenced to three years' imprisonment. When the end of his prison term was approaching, he was tried again on the same charges as previously and given another prison sentence of seven years. The years U Tin U spent in Insein Jail from 1989 to 1995 were his second stint in the infamous prison. His first period of incarceration had lasted from 1976 until 1980. U Tin U joined the army as a mere sixteen year old in 1943. After the war, he was included in the 150 Burmese officers to be given commissions in the reorganized Burma Army which formed the basis of the armed forces of the nation when it became independent. During the 1950s, he was twice decorated for valour shown in action against Kuomintang troops which had fled into Burma at the time of the communist victory in China. He rose rapidly from rank to rank through the 1960s and early 1970s, and in 1974 he was appointed Chief of Defence Services and Minister of Defence.

1974 was also the year when the meanness of spirit shown by the authorities over the funeral of U Thant, retired Secretary-General of the United Nations, scandalized the people of Burma and fermented anger among students already resentful of conditions imposed by the

Burmese Way to Socialism. In the course of disturbances related to this episode, and even more during the 1976 demonstrations by workers, U Tin U was hailed as a champion of the people. It is likely that his popularity with the public had much to do with his dismissal from the armed forces in March 1976. In September of the same year he was arrested, charged with alleged misprision of treason and sentenced to seven years' imprisonment.

On his release from prison under a general amnesty programme in 1980, U Tin U went straight to a monastery, where he stayed as a monk for two years. When he returned to lay life, he studied law and acquired the Registered Lawyers' certificate as well as the LL.B. degree. The democracy movement of 1988 drew him from a quiet private life into the struggle to bring justice and human rights to Burma. He was appointed Deputy Chairman of the NLD in September 1988, and in December of the same year he replaced U Aung Gyi as the Chairman of the party.

20. A Special Introduction

Four leading members of the Executive Committee of the NLD have already been introduced to the readers of 'Letters from Burma'. Now I would like to make a special introduction, to make known the only member of the original Executive Committee of the NLD who still remains in prison today: U Win Tin.

Unlike U Aung Shwe, U Kyi Maung, U Tin U and U Lwin, U Win Tin, born in 1930, was never a member of the armed forces. The world of letters was his domain. Even before graduation from university he had begun to work for the Burma Translation Society in the capacity of Assistant Editor. In 1954 he became Advisory Editor to a Dutch newspaper company. This was the beginning of a long career in journalism which culminated in his appointment as Chief Editor of the *Hanthawaddy*, one of the leading dailies of Burma.

The years during which U Win Tin was Chief Editor of the *Hanthawaddy* were years which saw the consolidation of the Burmese Way to Socialism. Progressive restrictions were placed on free speech and expression but a handful of writers and journalists quietly persisted in preserving their right to intellectual freedom. In 1978, a paper critical of the Burmese Way to Socialism was read at the Saturday Reading Circle of which U Win Tin was a leading member. As a consequence he was dismissed from his job and the *Hanthawaddy* newspaper was shut down by the authorities. For the next decade U Win Tin earned his living as a freelance writer and translator.

It was only natural that those who believed in intellectual freedom and justice should have been at the vanguard of the democracy movement which began in 1988. From the beginning U Win Tin played an active role in the Writers' Union that emerged during the early days of the movement. In September 1988, he became one of the secretaries of the Executive Committee of the NLD.

His undoubted ability and his strength of purpose made U Win Tin a prime target of those who opposed the democratic cause and in June 1989 he became one of the first leaders of the NLD to be arrested. The charge against him involved an unproven telephone conversation with the father of an individual who had been declared a fugitive from the law. Telephone conversations are, in any case, inadmissible as evidence under the law, but the law offers scant protection for those who challenge military rule in Burma. Immediately after his arrest, U Win Tin was kept without food and sleep for three days and interrogated about his activities in the democracy movement. It appeared that the interrogators wished to force him to admit that he was my adviser on political tactics, in other words, that he was my puppet master. A man of courage and integrity, U Win Tin would not be intimidated into making false confessions. In October 1989, he was sentenced to three years' imprisonment. In June 1992, a few months before his prison term was due to expire, he was submitted to another farcical trial and sentenced to an additional eleven years in jail.

U Win Tin is little given to talking about himself. As Secretary and General Secretary he and I worked together on an almost daily basis from the time the NLD was founded, but it was several months before I discovered, quite by chance, that he was a bachelor who lived alone and managed his own household chores. Soon after he was sentenced in 1989, the lease on his state-owned flat where he had been living for many years was cancelled and friends had to move his possessions out of the apartment.

U Win Tin's whole demeanour conveys such an impression of firmness that few people are aware that he suffers from a heart condition that requires constant medication. The long period spent in prison where medical care is inadequate and living conditions abysmal have aggravated his health problems. When US Congressman Bill Richardson saw him in February 1994 U Win Tin was wearing a neck support; spondylosis had been added to his afflictions. He was also in need of dental treatment. But his mind was as clear as ever and his spirit upright and unwavering. In the full knowledge that his every word would be reported to the authorities, he commented on the National Convention that had been arranged by the SLORC with his customary incisiveness and sent me a message of strong, unequivocal support.

Now U Win Tin is facing the serious possibility of a third sentence superimposed on the two that have already been slapped on him. Since November 1995, he and twenty-seven other political prisoners have been charged with breaking prison regulations and their trials are taking place within the jail precincts. The families of the defendants have asked the senior members of government, the Chief Justice and the Attorney General, to be allowed to provide the legal assistance entitled under the law. An answer has not yet been forthcoming.

21. Taking Tea

Tea plays a very important part in the social life of Burma. A pot of green tea, refilled again and again, is the hub of many an animated circle of conversation. There is also pickled tea leaves, *laphet*, soaked in good oil and served with such garnishes as sesame seeds, dried shrimps, roasted beans, peanuts and crisp fried garlic. It is indispensable as a traditional offering of hospitality, either as a conclusion to a meal or as a savoury snack to be taken with green tea in between meals.

While there is nothing more refreshing than a cup of pale amber tea made from roasted leaves grown in the Shan plateau, the Burmese people have become increasingly fond of 'sweet tea'. This is tea made with milk and sugar – but not in the English way. 'Sweet tea' stalls were originally run by Indian immigrants, so the tea is made in a way not unfamiliar to those who have frequented *char* shops in India. Tea leaves are boiled up with condensed milk in large vessels. The resulting pinkish brown beverage is thick and of a full flavour quite unknown to those who pour their tea into individual cups before adding a dainty splash of milk and restrained spoonfuls of sugar.

In Burmese teashops one does not ask for 'lapsang souchong' or Earl Grey or flowery orange pekoe or English breakfast blend. Instead one asks for 'mildly sweet', 'mildly sweet and strong', 'sweet and rich', or *Kyaukpadaung* (very sweet and thick). If the tea is made with imported condensed milk instead of the locally produced variety it becomes *she* ('special') and costs an extra couple of kyats.

Gathering with friends at teashops is so popular a pastime that the expression 'teashop sitting' is practically a verb in its own right. It is in teashops that people exchange news and, when it is not too dangerous an occupation, discuss politics. In fact there is an expression 'green tea circle' which implies an informal discussion group. There is even a little book of that title, based on a political column written between May 1946 and October 1947 by a famous newspaper man. The teashop is still one of the best places for catching up on the latest gossip around town, whether it is about the marital adventures of film stars or nefarious dealings in high circles.

Writers also go in for 'teashop sitting'. Sometimes such a gathering is the equivalent of an informal literary meeting or poetry reading. Students and other young people too congregate at favourite teashops to hold discussions ranging from pop music to political aspirations. Pungent catchwords and phrases often emerge from such teashop talk and quickly spread around town. These days there is a tacitly accepted dividing line between young people who go in for 'teashop sitting' and those who prefer to spend their leisure hours in discos and expensive restaurants. The difference between the two categories is to a considerable degree, but not altogether, financial. 'Teashop sitting' students are more in the tradition of those young men and women who turned Rangoon University into a bastion of the independence movement before the Second World War, while their disco-going counterparts tend to look upon the yuppie as their role model.

Taking a cup of tea is such a regular practice in Burma that, as in other Asian countries, a tip is known as 'tea money'. However, when the gap between the salaries earned by civil servants and the cost of living increased, the interpretation of the phrase 'tea money' underwent a metamorphosis. It came to mean bribes given to clear obstacles that block the bureaucratic process. But this was in the days when such bribes were relatively modest sums. Nowadays, when the going rate for speeding up a passport application is in five figures, 'tea money' is no longer a satisfactory euphemism for bribes: the current expression is 'pouring water', referring, one assumes, to the need for liberal 'libations' at all relevant departments.

The price of a cup of tea in an ordinary teashop is about eight to ten kyats, still not beyond the means of struggling writers and students. However, the cost of taking tea in one of the new, or newly renovated, starred hotels of Rangoon is quite beyond the dreams of most people in Burma. There, tea for a single person served in the English style costs three US dollars.

The official rate of exchange for one US dollar is less than six kyats but in recent weeks official exchange centres have been opened where Foreign Exchange Certificates (FECs) can be exchanged at the more realistic rate of 120 kyats to the dollar. This makes the price of taking a gracious cuppa in a luxury hotel equivalent to 360 kyats. Compare this to the basic monthly salary of the lowest echelon of civil servant, such as a junior policeman, which is 600 kyats, hardly sufficient to feed a family of four for a week. It is then easy to understand why the supplementary income needed by the government employees can no longer be adequately described by the expression 'tea money', even when the tea concerned is of the most expensive kind.

22. The Beautiful and the Ugly

Years ago, during a lesson on the Japanese tea ceremony at Oxford, our teacher showed us coloured slides of ceramic bowls fashioned by a master craftsman. The bowls had been photographed in the home of the master himself and the exquisite restraint of their beauty contrasted incongruously with the loud vulgarity of the modern carpet on which the master planted his feet and, consciously or unconsciously, feasted his eyes each day. Our teacher, an American who had lived and studied in Japan for many years to qualify as a master of the tea ceremony, laughed at our baffled expressions and remarked that some people only knew what was beautiful, they did not know what was ugly.

Our teacher spoke chiefly of aesthetic matters. He contrasted the clashing colours and rampant designs of elaborate brocades with the elegance of plain, dark fabrics printed with simple geometric patterns or discreet emblems; he compared garish neon-lit city areas with cool gardens of moss covered rocks and old pines. The tea ceremony with its spirit of *wakei seijaku* (harmony, respect, quietness and tranquillity) illustrated the necessity of removing all that is ugly or disharmonious before reaching out to a beauty that is both visual and spiritual.

The fundamental principle of aesthetics which we learnt from our teacher, that to acquire truly good taste one has to be able to recognize both ugliness and beauty, is applicable to the whole range of human experience. It is important to understand both what should be rejected and what should be accepted. I personally know many Japanese who are as ready to reject what is ugly as to accept what is beautiful. But I cannot help thinking that such a sense of discrimination is lacking in those who seek to promote business with Burma these days.

What do these advocates of precipitate economic engagement see when they look at our country? Perhaps they merely see the picturesque scenery, the instinctive smiles with which Burmese generally greet visitors, the new hotels, the cheap labour and what appear to them as golden opportunities for making money. Perhaps they do not know of the poverty in the countryside, the hapless people whose homes have been razed to make way for big vulgar buildings, the bribery and corruption that is spreading like a cancerous growth, the lack of equity that makes the so-called open-market economy very, very open to some and hardly ajar to others, the harsh and increasingly lawless actions taken by the authorities against those who seek democracy and human rights, the forced labour projects where men, women and children toil away without financial compensation under hard taskmasters in scenes reminiscent of the infamous railway of death during the Second World War.

It is surprising that those who pride themselves on their shrewdness and keen eye for opportunity cannot discern the ugly symptoms of a system that is undermining the moral and intellectual fibre and, consequently, the economic potential of our nation. If businessmen do not care about the numbers of political prisoners in our country, they should at least be concerned that the lack of an effective legal framework means there is no guarantee of fair business practice or, in cases of injustice, reparation. If businessmen do not care that our standards of health and education are deteriorating, they should at least be concerned that the lack of a healthy, educated labour force will inevitably thwart sound economic development. If businessmen do not care that we have to struggle with the difficulties of a system that gives scant attention to the well-being of the people, they should at least be concerned that the lack of necessary infrastructure and an underpaid and thereby corrupt bureaucracy hampers quick, efficient transactions. If businessmen do not care that our workers are exposed to exploitation, they should at least be concerned that a dissatisfied labour force will eventually mean social unrest and economic in-stability.

To observe businessmen who come to Burma with the intention of enriching themselves is somewhat like watching passers-by in an orchard roughly stripping off blossoms for their fragile beauty, blind to the ugliness of despoiled branches, oblivious of the fact that by their action they are imperilling future fruitfulness and committing an injustice against the rightful owners of the trees. Among these despoilers are big Japanese companies. But they do not represent the best of Japan. I have met groups of Japanese, both young and old, anxious to find out for themselves the true state of affairs in our country, prepared to look straight at both the beautiful and the ugly. At the weekend public meetings that take place outside my gate, there are usually a number of Japanese sitting in the broiling sun, who, although they cannot understand Burmese, pay close and courteous attention to all that is going on. And when, at the end of the meeting, many of them come up to me to say: *Gangatte kudasai* ('Hang in there and persevere!') I am strengthened by the knowledge that our struggle has the support of Japanese people in whom the sense of moral aesthetics is very much alive.

23. Old Songs

Some days ago two young Japanese women studying Burmese at Osaka University of Foreign Studies came to see me at a very opportune time. U Kyi Maung and I wanted help in translating a couple of Japanese songs. A few weeks ago U Kyi Maung had spoken at one of our weekend public meetings about these songs which he had learnt as a young soldier. Many of the songs of the armed forces of Burma date back to the days of the Second World War and have Burmese lyrics put to Japanese tunes. Thus the visitors from Japan who watch Burmese television today hear sounds associated with the days of militarist fascism and tend to ask with surprise or derision or both: 'Why do you play these old fascist songs in your country?'

U Kyi Maung explained that there was nothing intrinsically fascist about the original Japanese words of some of the songs and mentioned two which are well known in their Burmese versions. As I expressed an interest in learning more about such songs, he acquired from an old friend of his military academy days a couple of sheets of paper on which were printed, in pre-war style Japanese, a number of songs he had been taught as a young soldier.

With the help of the two young Japanese women we translated hesitatingly the words of a song entitled *Hohei no uta* (Infantry's Tune):

> The colour on my neckband is that of the blossom of the
>   many-branched sakura
> As the flowers of Yoshino drop in the wind,
> Those born as sons of Yamato
> Fall courageously in the front line like flowers.

The gun that measures one *shaku*[1] is no weapon.
A remnant of sword can achieve nothing.
It is the spirit of Yamato, instilled repeatedly
Beyond the realms of memory
Since over two thousand years ago,
That keeps two hundred thousand soldiers
In seventy stations,
Defending their flag,
Never surrendering their position,
Not even in their dreams.

And another song, *Aiba shingun ka* (March for my Lovely Horse):

How long ago is it since I left my country
Prepared to die together with this horse?
Old horse, are you feeling sleepy?
The reins I hold are as a vein that
Links your blood to mine.

What, U Kyi Maung queried, is there about such words that is fascist or even particularly militarist? An evocation of tender cherry blossoms, an emphasis on the spirit rather than on weapons, a sentimental ditty about an old horse. But because these songs were sung repeatedly as the Japanese army marched across Asia in obedience to the commands of a fascist military government, leaving devastation in its wake, the very tunes have come to be regarded as inauspicious sounds reverberating within the army; the soldier's discipline, self-sacrifice and love of nature, were wiped out by the deeds he was made to perform at the behest of leaders who had swept aside liberal values and chosen the way of military aggression to gain their ends, indifferent to the suffering of others.

27 March 1945 was the day when the people of Burma rose up in resistance against fascism. The NLD commemorated Fascist Resistance Day this year with a lecture at which several people spoke of their personal experiences during the resistance movement. The first speaker was Bohmu Aung, a hale octogenarian who had been one of the Thirty Comrades, a group of young men led by my father

who received military training from the Japanese army on Hainan Island in 1941. Then U Tin U and U Maung Maung Gyi, another member of the NLD, spoke of events during the early months of 1945 from the point of view of those who were at the time merely junior officers in the Burmese armed forces. The last two speakers at the lecture were a widely respected literary couple, U Khin Maung Latt and Daw Khin Myo Chit. Their modest and witty recollections of the part they as civilians had played in the resistance movement were particularly valuable. It reminded us of the crucial contribution made by the ordinary citizens of Burma toward the success of the struggle to free our country from both fascist domination and colonial rule. There are some things that we should not forget.

It is the love of ordinary people, in Burma, in Japan or anywhere else in the world, for justice and peace and freedom that is our surest defence against the forces of unreason and extremism that turn innocent songs into threatening war-chants.

1 A traditional measurement, equivalent to 30.3 centimetres.

24. Water Festival (1)

Poets who have known the disturbing beauty of Spring in temperate lands write about the month of April with a quivering nostalgia, fascinated, and perhaps a little frightened, by its uncertain glory. April in tropical Burma is of a totally different order from

> ... the cruellest month,
> Breeding lilacs out of the dead land,
> Stirring dull roots with spring rain.[1]

The cruelty of April in Burma lies not in the pain of returning life but in the searing heat and brassy glare of the sun that saps strength and energy, leaving people as parched and exhausted as the cracked earth. It is during this hot and draining month that the Burmese New Year falls. And fittingly the prelude to the New Year is a water festival.

The name of the festival is *Thingyan*. '*Thingyan*' denotes a changeover and the suffix '*maha*', great, is often added to indicate the major change from an old to a new year which the festival celebrates. We also use the suffix '*ata*', ending, as the festival actually takes place during the last four days of the old year, and the *ata* water that we pour on each other as part of the festivities symbolizes peace, prosperity and the washing away of impurities.

The form of the *Thingyan* festival has changed perceptibly over the last 200 years. An Englishman, Captain Symes, sent by the Viceroy of India on an embassy to the Burmese court at Ava in 1795, left a description of the water festival in which he took part:

To wash away the impurities of the past and begin the new year free from stain, women on this day throw water on every man they meet, and the men

95

are allowed to throw water on them in return. This permission to throw water on one another gives rise to a great deal of harmless merriment, especially amongst the young women, who, armed with large syringes or squirts and vessels, try to wet every man that goes along the street, and in their return receive a wetting with the utmost good nature.

The slightest indecency is never shown in this or in any other of their sports. Dirty water is never thrown. A man is not allowed to lay hold of a woman, but may throw as much water over her as he pleases, provided she has started first.[2]

The age of chivalry when only women were allowed to start throwing water first has long gone by. And these days hoses fitted with nozzles that spurt out strong jets of water have largely replaced syringes, squirts and dainty vessels. And many Burmese, especially those belonging to the older generation, would sadly admit that it can no longer be claimed that 'the slightest indecency is never shown' during the festival, especially since alcoholic excess has come to be associated with *thingyan*. In modern times it has become the practice to set up temporary buildings on the side of city streets for the purpose of throwing water and providing entertainment in the form of songs and dances. Carloads of merrymakers go from street to street getting wetter and wetter and in some cases getting more and more intoxicated.

But there is more to *Thingyan* than throwing water and having fun. It is a time for taking stock of the past year and using the last few days before the new year comes in to balance our 'merit book'. Some people spend the period of the water festival in meditating, worshipping at pagodas, observing the eight precepts,[3] releasing caged birds and fishes and performing other meritorious deeds. Children are told that Sakya comes down from his heavenly abode to wander in the human world during the days of *Thingyan*, carrying with him two large books, one bound in gold and the other bound in dog leather. The names of those who perform meritorious acts are entered in the golden book while the names of those who do not behave properly are noted down in the dog leather tome. It is especially important not to get angry during *Thingyan* or to make others angry.

It is therefore considered wrong to throw water over anybody who is unwilling to be doused.

There are special foods associated with *Thingyan*. One of the most popular of these are small boiled rice dumplings with a stuffing of palm sugar, eaten with a sprinkling of shredded fresh coconut. Often hot chillies are put in place of the palm sugar in a few dumplings and there is much good humoured laughter when some unfortunate bites into one of these lethal sweetmeats and vociferously expresses his chagrin. Because it is such a hot time of the year, sweet, cooling drinks made from coconut milk, swirling with bits of rice pasta tinted a pale green, sago, seaweed jelly and other garnishes are served as part of the festivities.

A traditional part of the water festival has disappeared in recent years: the *Thingyan thangyat*, rhyming choruses that provide pungently witty commentaries on topical subjects, particularly on the government. It was a way of allowing people to let off steam healthily once a year and also a way of allowing sensible governments to find out how the people truly feel about them. But the SLORC is incapable of coping with criticism. Members of the NLD who sang such choruses in 1989 were imprisoned.

---

1 *The Waste Land*, T. S. Eliot (London, 1922).

2 *An Account of an Embassy to the Kingdom of Ava: Sent by the Governor-General of India in the Year 1795* (London, 1800).

3 To undertake the Eight Precepts is to abstain from taking life, taking what is not given, wrong conduct in sexual desires, telling lies, drinking alcohol, taking solid food after midday, dressing in any colour but plain white, and sleeping in high or big beds.

25. Water Festival (2)

This year *Thingyan*, the water festival that takes place at the end of the Burmese lunar year, began on 12 April. On that day, in the midst of a flurry of activities connected with the ceremonies the NLD were planning for the 14th, we arranged an *ata* pot. This is an earthenware vessel filled with symbolic leaves and flowers for the purpose, some say, of welcoming Sakya when he comes down for the water festival. Others see it as an insurance against bad luck, particularly for those who were born on the day of the week on which the last day of *Thingyan* falls, as such people are held to be highly vulnerable to misfortune during the year to come. Whatever the original purpose may have been, placing the *ata* pot in an auspicious part of the house is generally seen as an indispensable part of the preparations for *Thingyan*.

The flower especially associated with the water festival is the *padauk* (the Indian or Malabar Kino), bright yellow with a very sweet but light fragrance. It usually blooms at this time of year after a shower of rain, but as the second week of April was quite dry we had resigned ourselves to a *Thingyan* without the enchanting sight of frothy golden blooms adorning all and sundry. However on the day of our NLD water festival somebody brought some *padauk* which had been found in bloom on some eccentric tree and I was able to tuck a happy spray into my hair.

In Arakan on the western coast of Burma, *Thingyan* is celebrated in a particularly refined and charming way. Therefore we arranged our water-throwing somewhat along Arakanese lines although we could not observe all their beautiful *Thingyan* traditions. Three long wooden boats were filled with water and young women stood behind the boats armed with bowls in which they scooped up water to throw at the young men who queued up to stand opposite them, behind a barrier of bamboo poles. To throw back water in their turn the young men had to try to catch, in small cups provided for them, the water thrown by the young women. Of course the whole arrangement was blatantly in favour of the young women who were able to keep up a relentless deluge. Whoever ducked his head or turned away his face or wiped it or shielded it in any way was held to have surrendered. It must be admitted there were very few surrenders although the young men were barely able to collect enough water in their cups to enable them to return the fire. Each water battle lasted for one minute. A whistle would be blown to indicate that time was up and one dripping and bedraggled batch of water warriors would make way for another. Those who were not content with a single bout of water throwing would go straight out to stand in queue for another round. There were many indefatigable spirits who spent most of the day by the water boats, taking a rest only at the hottest time of the afternoon when play was stopped for a short period.

At the same time as the water throwing was going on, there was an almost continuous programme of songs and dances for the entertainment of those who wanted to sit and dry out. Most of the dances had been hastily rehearsed by amateurs and could not have been described as examples of choreographic perfection. But imbued with the generous spirit of the season, the audience were quite determined to be pleased and even the most fastidious of them willingly overlooked all flaws.

The main purpose of our *Thingyan* celebrations was to collect funds for political prisoners. There was a stall where NLD souvenirs were sold, a hot drinks stall, a stall selling pickled tea and ginger preparations and a stall where a substantial Burmese meal could be bought at a very reasonable price. A Burmese meal basically consists of what Japanese would describe as *kare-raisu* (curry and rice), although our curries are considerably different from the *kare* that is served in Japan. During the days of *Thingyan* many Burmese eat vegetarian food as an act of merit, so a variety of both vegetarian and non-vegetarian curries were provided at our food stall. The exercise involved in wielding bowls, buckets and syringes and the sheer exhilaration of a good drenching when the temperature is in the nineties give a sharp edge to one's appetite. It was little wonder our food stalls did a very brisk trade and sold out early.

There is a lovely Burmese custom known as *satuditha*. This is a Pali expression meaning the four directions, and *satuditha* is the charitable act of offering free food or drink to those who come from the four points of the compass, that is to say, to all comers. For our *Thingyan* celebrations NLD members from various townships in the Rangoon division had provided seasonal sweets and cool drinks as *satuditha*. It was a pleasure to watch the faces of those at the *satuditha* stall; their expressions were such a striking illustration of mutual joy and satisfaction. We believe *satuditha* results in spiritual benefits not only for those who offer it but also for those who accept the offering because by accepting it they help the others acquire merit. Moreover, it is held that partaking of *satuditha* offerings during *Thingyan* brings good health in the new year.

26. Water Festival (3)

The energy of the young is wonderful. The NLD *Thingyan* festival had begun at eight o'clock in the morning and concluded at five o'clock in the afternoon according to plan. After the visitors had left, the young helpers who had been on the go all day but who were still overflowing with vim insisted that we oldies engage in a bout of water throwing with them. So we took our places on the young women's side of the water boats and together with the girls and children tried to splash the young men into submission. Scooping up water in bowlfuls at top speed and throwing it at stoically laughing young men is strenuous work. We participated in three rounds, one at each boat, and ended up drenched to the skin, invigorated and exhausted. In spite of our best efforts only one young man could have been said to have clearly 'surrendered' as he held up his cap in front of his face to ward off our liquid barrage.

As far as I was concerned, one such day of water throwing was quite enough to last us for at least another year but of course the young people saw things in a different light. Before they had even finished tidying up for the evening they were making plans to establish a little water-throwing depot on the side of the street in front of our garden the next day. As that would be the last day of the water festival, they were determined to make the most of it.

Equipped with large tanks of water, diverse vessels, syringes and several cassettes of *Thingyan* songs, our band of water players took up position outside the front gates next morning. The star of the show was a small seven year old. Deceptively frail-looking with long hair, sweetly pouting lips, round cheeks and thin legs, this little girl had more stamina than most boys. She had been engaged in dousing others or getting doused herself almost without respite since the first day of *Thingyan*, yet she was unflagging on the fourth and last day and outlasted almost everybody else.

It gave me a sense of deep contentment to work quietly by myself inside the house while faint sounds of music and laughter and the shrill shouts of children drifted in from the road. To be able to clear my desk of accumulated work and to know that our young people were having a happy time afforded double satisfaction. The water throwers occasionally wandered into the house, faces glowing from their exertions, leaving a trail of wet footprints, getting themselves something to eat. During the hottest part of the day they took a rest to recharge their batteries for the final onslaught, then went back out to join the watery fray with new vigour.

In the late afternoon, our water throwers asked me to join them. On the understanding that I would not participate in the action, as I was feeling none too robust after the activities of the previous day, I went out to observe the proceedings. Two young men with whistles signalled to passing cars filled with soaking wet people to indicate that those who wanted to have a go at getting even wetter should stop. The cars usually stopped and with good humour the passengers allowed our water throwers to get to work. Some of our young people had begun to slow down but the hardiest ones, including of course our seven year old, gave an impressive demonstration of their capacity for sustained endeavour.

It was obvious that many of those cruising around in cars for the joy of exposing themselves to as much *Thingyan* water as possible had imbibed freely. Inebriated merrymakers often make provocative remarks or crude gestures and get involved in brawls quite out of keeping with the traditional spirit of the New Year season. But such unseemly behaviour was not at all evident in those who stopped for our water throwers. Everybody was cheerful and friendly and even those who were evidently tipsy did not fail in courtesy. The single exception was a man who jumped down unsteadily from a car with a bottle of liquor in one hand and in the other an aerosol can from which he sent out sprays of scent. He became aggressive when he was asked to contain his overwhelming enthusiasm.

Of course it was not all sweetness and light everywhere throughout the festival. Apart from the inevitable brawls that break out when spirits are running too high, a number of traffic incidents resulting in loss of life and limb take place every year. This year too was not free from the usual quota of casualties. There were also a few unnecessary incidents involving NLD caps which had been sold at our ceremony on the 14th. Young men (wearing such caps), some of whom were not even members of the NLD, were harassed by the authorities. One young man was beaten, then dragged off under arrest while his assailant was left untouched.

In spite, or perhaps because of, the repression and injustices to which they are subjected, the Burmese have a remarkable capacity for extracting the maximum amount of fun from the opportunities offered to them during our traditional festivals.

27. A Fishy Episode

It is traditional to release caged birds or fish on Burmese New Year's Day as an act of merit. In April 1989, the last Burmese New Year I celebrated before my house arrest, we released some doves, launching them into the emptiness above the Inya Lake on which my house stands. The poor creatures had become used to captivity and fluttered about in a dazed way before they gained enough confidence to take off. One fell into the reeds at the edge of the lake and had to be rescued and relaunched. It hovered uncertainly near us for a few minutes before soaring away into the distance. We hoped that its flight would not end in the snare of a bird catcher. Many released birds are caught again and again and sold and resold to those who wish to gain the merit of freeing caged creatures. I could not help wondering how much value there could be to a gesture of liberation that does not truly guarantee freedom.

This year the women's wing of the NLD decided they would like to arrange a fish-releasing ceremony on New Year's Day, 16 April. They would gather at my house and walk in procession to a pond near the Shwedagon Pagoda where the fish could be released to swim their lives out in peace. The Rangoon Division Law and Order Restoration Council (LORC) was informed of our plan before the beginning of the water festival which precedes the New Year. On 15 April, the authorities reacted. A number of township NLD offices received letters from their respective LORCs forbidding them to go ahead with the ceremony. In addition U Aung Shwe, the Chairman of the NLD, and two of the members of the Executive Committee were asked to come to the office of the Bahan Township LORC. A statement was read out: the government could not allow the NLD ceremony to take place; as the ceremony would be conducted in the form of a public gathering organized by a political party, it would have to be considered a political activity and the authorities could not allow political benefit to be derived from a traditional ceremony. Further, such a gathering would be detrimental to peace and harmony, to the rule of law and to the prevalence of order. It would disturb and destroy peace and harmony in the nation and incite fear and alarm. U Aung Shwe countered that the whole statement was based on mere assumptions and left a written protest.

The reaction of the authorities was both nonsensical and revealing. The SLORC makes repeated claims that they have succeeded in restoring law and order and peace and harmony to the land. How fragile must be the law and order that can be seriously threatened by a procession of women taking part in a traditional religious ceremony. How unsubstantial must be the peace and harmony in a country where such a procession is expected to throw the populace into a panic. We knew that what the authorities really feared was not so much a public disturbance as a demonstration of public support for the NLD. However, New Year's Day should be an auspicious occasion and we wished it to be a day of happiness rather than confrontation, so we cancelled our plans for the releasing of fish. We would listen to the chanting of protective sutras and pay our respects to our elders. But the authorities had other plans.

On New Year's Day at about 11.30 in the morning, the street in front of my house was blocked off with barbed-wire barricades. Nobody was allowed to come in or go out except members of the security forces and numbers of awkward-looking men in civilian clothes, each with a handkerchief tied around one wrist. We discovered later that these were members of the Union Solidarity and Development Association (USDA). They had been collected from various townships and told to beat up those members of the NLD who came in through the barricades. The USDA were assured that the authorities would be behind them. Once serious fighting had erupted, all those involved would be taken away to prison (there were several prison vans waiting at the local police station), but USDA members would soon be released. The NLD members would no doubt be given substantial prison sentences. Thus, the USDA was 'promoted' from mere tomato throwers to thugs. (In 'An Eventful Week' I wrote about an aborted plan to throw tomatoes at us; on that occasion USDA members had rubber bands around their wrists as an identifying mark.)

The planned violence did not materialize because the NLD members took a firm, disciplined stand. They did not rush the barricades but they refused to leave on the orders of the security forces. They waited for a decision to be taken by the members of the Executive Committee who had been allowed to come to my house. We decided that the ceremony of paying our respects to the elders must go ahead; if our people were prevented from coming to us, we would go out to them. Accordingly, we walked out through the barricades to where our people stood and thus an auspicious New Year's Day ceremony took place in the middle of the street, near a crossroad. It seemed an omen that the NLD would not lack public attention during the coming year.

28. Repairing the Roof

There is a Burmese saying to the effect that if the roof is not sound the whole house becomes vulnerable to leaks. That is to say, if soundness is lacking at the top there are bound to be problems all down the line to the very bottom.

It has certainly been my personal experience over a number of monsoon seasons that a leaking roof renders other improvements to a house futile. During the six months of rain, every spare basin, bucket, saucepan and plastic container in my house has to be commandeered to catch the rivulets that flow in merrily. When there is an especially heavy downpour the containers have to be emptied frequently and the myriad of small leaks that appear quite suddenly (and disappear just as suddenly) at unexpected places have to be mopped up.

Keeping the inside of the house dry becomes a constant juggling act with a variety of vessels and rags. I tried to stop the incessant drips with intricate arrangements of plastic sheets, waterproof tape, putty and other gummy substances. But all the manoeuvres succeeded merely in stemming the torrent temporarily and over the years paint, plaster and woodwork in the paths of the worst leaks steadily deteriorated.

So making the roof rainproof was at the top of the priority list of essential repairs that we decided had to be undertaken during the dry season. Only when the roof was sound would it be worthwhile to put new paint on walls that have been neglected for several decades and, in general, to make the house cleaner and brighter.

There were some who had the, in my view, horrifying idea of replacing the original tile roof with a corrugated-iron one, but I held out firmly for reusing the old tiles and supplementing those that had been damaged beyond redemption with other ones. As soon as the tiles were brought down from the roof the advocates of corrugated iron were totally won over. Each tile was solid and beautifully crafted, and baked into it were the name of the company that had produced it, the date (1936, presumably the year the house was built) and a number.

The tiles fit so well into each other that in one part of the roof where the supporting woodwork had rotted away, a sheet of tiles as firmly linked together as the best Lego model had managed to keep in place. And once they had been washed clean the tiles glowed a soft red and looked as good as new. I must confess some of us waxed quite lyrical over the beauty and durability of the tiles.

Of course, there were a number that were broken or too badly chipped to be reused so we had to buy replacements from shops that specialized in selling parts of old buildings that had been pulled down. The tiles that we managed to get were slightly different from our original ones, but were equally well-crafted and almost as solid and on each of them was the date: 1865. We viewed them with awe and could not help remarking that we human beings, often so proud of our powers and achievements, are not even as durable as a simple brick tile.

For all the metaphors about human clay, in substance we are probably closer to wood. Many of the wooden supports in the house had not been able to withstand the onslaught of the seasons, despite the fact that only teak had been used. Considering present day prices there was no question of putting in new teak supports. Even old teak in the quantities we needed was prohibitively expensive so we decided on old *pyinkadoe* (iron wood), which came, like the nineteenth-century tiles, from buildings that had been pulled down in recent years. The builders thought that with proper maintenance the supports fashioned from the old wood should be good for another sixty years.

Repairing the roof involves reorganizing the whole house. I had to keep moving around from room to room as the builders kept removing the tiles. The very day after the first lot of tiles had been removed it rained. Not only buckets and basins and pots and pans were brought into operation, there were even a few glass tumblers catching solitary drips. The most abiding impression of the episode was the camaraderie and laughter with which everybody rallied around, viewing the somewhat unseasonable rain not so much as a setback but as a comic interlude. Into each life some rain must fall, and how good when its fall contributes to a better atmosphere. For me there was a special bonus: I had moved, together with some bulky furniture, into the hottest room of the house but thanks to the rain it was pleasantly cool for most of the time I had to camp there.

While the repairs on the house were going on life was doubly hectic as I had to cope not only with my routine political work but also with packing and unpacking, tidying and rearranging furniture. It occurred to me more than once how important was the contribution of the wives of my male colleagues. By looking after all household matters and supplying endless encouragement to their menfolk these indomitable women, to whom the international media pay scant attention, play an essential role in our endeavours to repair the roof of our nation.

29. Rain Thoughts

The word 'monsoon' has always sounded beautiful to me, possibly because we Burmese, who are rather inclined to indulge in nostalgia, think of the rainy season as most romantic.

As a child, I would stand on the veranda of the house where I was born and watch the sky darken and listen to the grown-ups wax sentimental over smoky banks of massed rain clouds. When the rain came down in rods of glinting crystal, a musically inclined cousin would chant, 'Oh, the golden rain is brown,' a line from a popular song. I could not make up my mind whether the words were poetic or comic, but I was ready to accept that it was an apt description as I had often seen raindrops shoot out sparks of gold when hit by stray sunbeams against a sky bruised with shades of brown. I was also quite willing to go along with the adult contention that falling rain stirs undefined yearnings for times past even though as a six year old I could not have claimed much of a past. It seemed very grown up to regard a soft grey day of the monsoons with an appropriate expression of inexplicable sorrow.

One of the first poems I learned, written by our great poet Min Thu Wun and known to almost every Burmese child, was about the rains: 'In the months of Wahso and Wagaung when the waters are high, let us go and gather the ripe *thabye* fruit . . .' I would ask my mother for some *thabye* fruit (*Eugenia jambolana*) just to see what it was like, but it was scarce in Rangoon and I did not come across one solitary specimen. It was only during my teens when I accompanied my mother to India that she was able to provide me with this fruit that had been so much a part of the poetic imagination of my childhood. 'This,' she said one day, handing me a bulging packet, with the radiant smile that put the tiniest of dimples at one corner of her mouth, 'this is the *thabye* fruit I could not get for you when you were a child'.

In Delhi, the fruit was called *jamu*, and when it was in season it would be gathered in enormous baskets under the trees at the corner of the street where we lived. The shape and size of large olives with a shiny dark purple skin, the *jamu* had a sweet, astringent-tasting flesh that left bright magenta stains on the tongue and lips. It was as exotic as I had imagined it would be in the days when I chanted the poems as I hopped around under a monsoon shower squelching mud between my toes, a thin brown urchin delighting in the cool, clean feel of the rain and the sense of freedom. When bathing in the rain was no longer one of the great pleasures of my existence, I knew I had left my childhood behind me.

There is another bit of poetry about the *thabye* fruit and the rain quite different from Min Thu Wun's happy evocation of small boys and girls valiantly tramping through thorny bushes and braving leeches to find a trove of delicious fruit. It is usually recited in mournful tone in keeping with Burmese sentiment about the sadness of falling rain:

> The *thabye* is in fruit, the waters are in flood,
> Today the toddy nuts are falling, the rain is unceasing;
> Oh, Ko Datha, I long to go back to mother;
> Show me the way . . .

This is based on the Buddhist story of Padasari, the daughter of rich parents who ran away to a far place with one of her house slaves. After bearing two sons, she was filled with such longing to see her parents that she asked her husband to take her back home. On the journey, she lost her husband and both children in a series of tragic incidents. She managed to continue on to the land where her parents lived only to discover that her whole family – father, mother, and brother – had died and had just been cremated. The unfortunate young woman lost her mind and wandered around in a state of mad grief until the Lord Buddha taught her how to achieve peace of mind. Padasari is seen as the epitome of the consuming fire of extreme grief. But her tale is essentially one of supreme joy: the joy of victory over the self. There are many pictures that depict Padasari's frantic despair at the loss of her husband and sons, often against a backdrop of rain and storm. On the surface it is not a scene calculated to induce much enthusiasm for wet weather, but because we know that the ultimate outcome is a happy one, it does not really dampen one's spirits.

Once more the monsoons have come to Burma, the cooling rain bringing relief from the broiling heat of April. At this time six years ago, the first democratic general election in thirty years was held in our country. The people of Burma went to the polls with an exemplary sense of responsibility and discipline, buoyed up by the hope that after three decades of authoritarian misrule they would at last achieve a system that ensured respect for their collective will. Their hopes were cruelly dashed. The results of the election have been ignored and Burma remains subject to the whims of a small élite. Our struggle for a nation ruled in accordance with democratic principles continues, refreshed and re-energized by the new season.

30. Eight Years Ago

In Burma the number eight is not generally held to be in any way special, although as Buddhists most of the people of the country know of the Noble Eightfold Path and the eight victories of Lord Buddha. But eight years ago, in 1988, the number eight unexpectedly acquired a potent political significance. On the eighth of August of that year, '8–8–88', a general strike was declared and public demonstrations that had been taking place throughout the nation for several days took on massive proportions. Participating in these peaceful demonstrations were people of all ages, from all different strata of society: students, farmers, labourers, civil servants, including members of the armed forces, Buddhist monks, Christians, Muslims, intellectuals, professionals, businessmen, small traders, housewives and artists. Their united demand was for change: they wanted no more of the authoritarian rule, initiated by a military coup in 1962, that had impoverished Burma intellectually, politically, morally and economically.

The discontent that had been simmering in the country for years had come to a boil in March 1988 after an incident in a tea shop led to the killing of a university student by members of the security forces. Students held demonstrations demanding an open investigation into the death, and when it became evident that these demands would not be met by the authorities, more demonstrations broke out in June. The country was in ferment and in July U Ne Win, the Chairman of the Burma Socialist Programme Party (BSPP), U San Yu, the President, and a number of the nation's top leaders resigned. At the dramatic emergency Congress where the resignations were announced, the outgoing Chairman declared that a decision should be made as to whether the country should continue under one-party rule or whether it should opt for a multi-party system. He also made the ominous remark that when the army shot, it shot straight.

Within a matter of days it became sufficiently clear that the new administration under President U Sein Lwin had no intention of abolishing one-party dictatorship. The frustrations that the people of Burma had been holding back for some two decades erupted and they poured out on to the streets in a great, spontaneous demonstration of their desire for a governing system that would respect their will. The movement for democracy had begun.

It is never easy to convince those who have acquired power forcibly of the wisdom of peaceful change. On the night of 8 August the army moved to crush the demonstrations, shooting down thousands of unarmed people, including children, throughout the land. The killings went on for four days, but the demonstrations continued and the president, U Sein Lwin, resigned. The next president, Dr Maung Maung, was the first head of state Burma had known in nearly three decades who had not come into government from the ranks of the military. For a while the people hoped their demands for democracy would be met speedily. However, on 18 September troops once again fired on unarmed demonstrators and the military took over the administration of the country. The new junta assumed what has often been described as an Orwellian title: the State Law and Order Restoration Council or SLORC.

The SLORC proclaimed that it was not interested in holding on to power for long and that it would establish multi-party democracy in Burma within a short period of time. Political parties were required to register with the Multi-party Elections Commission which was charged with the responsibility of organizing free and fair elections. More than 200 parties registered, among them the National League for Democracy (NLD).

From the very beginning the path the NLD had to tread was far from smooth. The enthusiastic support of the public which led to NLD offices springing up even in the remotest villages brought upon the party the unfriendly attention of the authorities. The SLORC had announced that the military powers would observe a strictly neutral position but it soon became evident that the National Unity Party, as the BSPP had decided to restyle itself, was very much the favoured political organization. Harassment and intimidation became everyday matters for members of the NLD. But we learned to cope and amidst teething problems our party became stronger by the day.

In building up the NLD our chief concern was to establish a close, mutually beneficial relationship with the general public. We listened to the voice of the people, that our policies might be in harmony with their legitimate needs and aspirations. We discussed with them the problems of our country and explained why, in spite of its inevitable flaws, we considered democracy to be better than other political systems. Most important of all, we sought to make them understand why we believed that political change was best achieved through non-violent means.

31. A Dissident's Life (1)

Life is seldom dull for dissidents in Burma. I just looked up 'dissident' in three different dictionaries and the definition I like best is 'one who disagrees with the aims and procedures of the government'. That about sums up the position of the NLD and others working for democracy in Burma: we disagree with the present aims and procedures of the SLORC. Agreeing to disagree is a prerogative only of those who live under a democratic system. Under an authoritarian regime, disagreeing can be seen as a crime. This makes life for us rather difficult. Sometimes dangerous. But certainly not dull.

The main issue on which we disagree with SLORC is the matter of promises. We hold that a promise given to the nation should be honoured, not cast aside with a shrug and a sneer when 'it no longer suits them'. When the military regime took over power in September 1988 it announced that it had no intention of governing the country for a long period. It would assume the responsibility of bringing genuine multi-party democracy to Burma and power would be transferred to the party that proved victorious in 'free and fair elections'. The elections of May 1990 were hailed as one of the freest and fairest ever and the NLD won 82 per cent of the seats. As this was not the result SLORC had expected it decided to forget its earlier promise and brought out Notification 1/90 (another nice Orwellian touch), according to which the job of the elected representatives was merely to draw up a state constitution. But once the NLD and other political parties had been made to sign an undertaking to abide by this notification, SLORC proceeded to organize a National Convention in which less than one fifth of the delegates were elected representatives of the people. The duty of the Convention was to endorse the basic principles of the state constitution which had been laid down by the authorities without reference to public sentiment.

It has been recognized by successive resolutions of the United Nations General Assembly that the will of the people of Burma expressed through the elections of 1990 remains valid. In May, on the sixth anniversary of the elections, the NLD decided to organize a conference of its elected representatives. This would have been a simple enough matter in countries where political parties are allowed to operate as genuine political organizations. Not so in Burma. Even the day-to-day running of an NLD office requires perseverance, patience, ingenuity and cool nerves. To begin with, a landlord who rents out office space to the NLD would be told that his house or apartment could be sealed off or confiscated at any time the authorities consider that the activities of the party justify such a move. Thus finding a place to use as a party office is the first hurdle that has to be overcome, giving members of the NLD much practice in political education and friendly persuasion. In some places the NLD has been obliged to move its office several times because of pressure exerted on landlords. In others the NLD was made to shift its office from a main road to a back street so its presence would not be so obvious.

The presence of an NLD office is generally made known by its signboard. And there is quite a saga attached to the signboards. When political parties were allowed to register with the Multi-party Elections Commission in 1988, they were also allowed to put up party signboards on the exterior walls or perimeter of their offices. But after a few months, during which bright red and white NLD signboards blossomed all over Burma from big cities to forgotten little hamlets deep in the countryside, it was announced that no party signboards should be put up in offices at the village and ward level. The reason given was that a multiplicity of party signboards in small villages and wards would lead to clashes among members of the respective parties. This was unconvincing as no such clashes had taken place and in many villages and wards the NLD was the only party with an office and a signboard. We discussed the matter with the commission and a compromise was reached. Signboards would be allowed in village and ward offices which had already put them up before, if I remember the date correctly, 16 December 1988.

But there are still villages and wards where the decision of the Commission has been ignored by the local authorities and NLD offices are still continuing the struggle to be allowed to put up signboards outside their usually very modest premises. There are places where NLD offices have been told to reduce the size of their signboards. There have been cases where local authorities have objected to NLD offices putting back signboards that had been temporarily removed for renovation. There have been instances of local authorities forcing NLD offices to remove their signboards; recently in some towns in the Irrawaddy Division, members of the local Red Cross and the Union Solidarity and Development Association have joined in these operations. Where else in the world has the matter of putting up a party signboard turned into an open-ended saga?

32. A Dissident's Life (2)

In Burma, one should approach the telephone with a prayer on the lips and determination to try, try and try again. Getting through to the required number at the first attempt is such a rare occurrence that it is an event to greet with incredulity and an expression of thanks to all powers, seen and unseen. The post office is no more reliable than the telephone system. I cannot quite make up my mind whether so many letters addressed to me fail to arrive because of the inefficiency of the post office or because of the efficiency of the Military Intelligence. My dear Japanese teacher Michiko-san sent me a little note through somebody who came to Rangoon to let me know she has been writing to me regularly through the post. None of these letters has reached me. Other friends also send messages to tell me they have written but their letters have not arrived either. Lately, the authorities have even prohibited courier services from delivering magazines and papers addressed to me.

With such unreliable communication services, inviting people from all over Burma to an NLD conference in Rangoon is not something that can be done with ease by a secretary sitting at a desk. It requires time and organization. It was therefore not surprising that some of our elected representatives found security personnel on their doorstep before they had even received invitations to the conference. The representatives were asked if they intended to attend the conference and when they answered 'yes' they were whisked off to detention.

During the week before the conference was scheduled to take place, nearly 300 elected representatives were arrested. In the face of the protests by the NLD and an international outcry, SLORC claimed that the representatives had merely been taken in for questioning and would be released shortly. This statement was partly correct: our representatives were certainly questioned. There were variations in the questions asked from one part of the country to the other but there were some which came up everywhere: why was the NLD holding this conference? Was the party going to set up a parallel government? How did the representatives assess the current political situation? What were their political beliefs? How did they think the situation had changed since my release from house arrest? What was their opinion of SLORC? What did they think of its aims and achievements? Did they think dialogue was possible between the NLD and SLORC? What did they think were the chances of success for such a dialogue?

It seemed to us that the authorities were unnecessarily nervous about the idea of the NLD carrying out its routine work as a political organization. We saw no reason why a conference of some 300 people should be viewed as an event which would create chaos and throw the country into confusion. We decided to adapt the plans in accord with the situation. As the great majority of our elected representatives were in detention, we decided that we would expand the conference to a congress, the first of a series which would lay down a future work programme for our party.

In addition to our elected representatives, the authorities had also taken into custody a number of party workers and members of my office staff. Other party workers rallied around to fill the gaps that had been left and preparations for the Congress proceeded in an atmosphere that was a cross between a crusade and a carnival, with everybody determined to keep faith with those who had been arrested by making a success of the occasion. The people also rallied around to demonstrate their solidarity. On the weekend of the Congress our usual public meetings outside my house were attended by record numbers of supporters in spite of the inclement weather.

The three days of the Congress went by quickly, leaving us all exhausted but thoroughly satisfied with what had been accomplished in the face of so much harassment and intimidation. But this was not the end of the story. A few days after the Congress was over the authorities started releasing those who had been arrested. We then learned there had been a systematic campaign to try to make our elected representatives relinquish their status as members of parliament and to give up their membership in our party. To some it was merely suggested that such steps would be desirable but there were cases where pressure was exerted. There were threats of prison sentences, loss of business opportunities, evictions from state-owned apartments, dismissal from their jobs of family members who belonged to the civil service.

NLD workers are often 'reminded' of the possible consequences of continued involvement in politics. In the middle of the night there could be a pounding on the door that signals arrest. Members of the security services could be lying in wait at a dark corner of a market place, ready to pounce. Life is certainly not dull for dissidents in Burma.

33. A Friend in Need

Many indeed are the uses of adversity, and one of the most valuable is the unique opportunity it offers for discovering little-known aspects of the human society in which we live. The experience gained by those of us who have borne the full force of state persuasion is not always comfortable, but it is very enriching. Injustice and cruelty are transformed from the ingredients of a ripping drama to the hazards of everyday existence.

Once poetic concepts such as villainy and honour, cowardice and heroism, become common currency, the stuff of epics is lived through from day to day. Duplicity and treachery cease to be merely the vivid creations of imaginative writers and become instead the trappings of families who have basked in one's affections and partaken freely of one's goodwill. The kiss of Judas is no longer just a metaphor, it is the repeated touch of cool perfidy on one's own cheek. Those held in trust and esteem show themselves capable of infinite self-deception as they seek to deceive others. Spines ostensibly made of steel soften and bend like wax in the heat of a high Burmese summer.

The man stripped of all props except that of his spirit is sounding not only the depths he is capable of plumbing, but also testing the heights that he can scale. An individual who appears weak turns out to possess adamantine qualities. The easy-going 'featherweight' demonstrates a solid capacity for self-sacrifice and integrity.

The most indifferent seeming character unexpectedly proves to be a fountain of warmth and kindness: a caring, meticulous nursemaid to those suffering physical pain or mental anguish. The glaring light of adversity reveals all the rainbow hues of the human character and brings out the true colours of people, particularly of those who purport to be your friends.

There is an anthology of pithy sayings, the *Lokaniti*, which has traditionally been regarded in Burma as a guide to prudent behaviour. It is a combination of shrewd observations and moral principles intended to help us negotiate the pitfalls of worldly existence. The section of the *Lokaniti* devoted to friendship displays a fair degree of cynicism: 'In poverty a friend forsakes you; son and wife, and brother too forsake you; being rich, they cling to you. Wealth in this world is a great friend.' Then there is a definition of friendship which would set those who run the gamut of the vicissitudes of political struggle in Burma nodding their heads vigorously in agreement: 'The friends who stand by you in severe ailment, in time of scarcity, or in misfortune, when captured by an enemy, at a king's door, or in the charnel-house, they indeed are good friends.'

During the hectic days of late May and early June, when a series of critical political events were triggered off by the arrests of the NLD members elected to parliament, a stream of foreign correspondents came to find out how we were coping with the situation. One of them commented on the fact that we did not appear to be unhappy. 'U Tin U is smiling broadly and U Kyi Maung is cracking jokes,' he said. 'Why are you not in a state of distress? Isn't the situation rather grim?' I suppose some would have seen the situation as grim, but to us, it was just another challenge; and the knowledge that we were facing it together with proven friends was simple reason for good cheer.

A doctor once recommended thinking happy thoughts as a most effective remedy for diverse illnesses. Certainly one of the happiest of thoughts is one's friends; old friends with whom you have shared youthful dreams of an ideal world, new friends with whom you are striving to achieve a realistic version of that ideal. It is comforting to know that friends you have not met for several decades, leading secure lives in countries where their rights are protected by the law, care as much for your welfare now as they did in the days when the Beatles were young and you argued over Dag Hammerskjöld's *Markings*. Friends telephone across continents and oceans to find out how I am and to exchange news.

We never talk about anything world shaking, never discuss anything out of the ordinary, we just make conventional enquiries about each other's health and families and a few light-hearted remarks about the current situation. But each unimportant conversation is a solemn confirmation of friendship. I have a friend who, if I happen to be too busy to take the call, leaves a simple message: 'Tell her I called.' It is enough to dissolve all the cares of the day.

According to the teachings of Buddhism, a good friend is one who gives things hard to give, does what is hard, bears hard words, tells you his secrets, guards your secrets assiduously, does not forsake you in times of want and does not condemn you when you are ruined. With such friends, one can travel the roughest road and not be defeated by hardship. Indeed, the rougher the path, the greater the delight in the company of *kalyanamitta*, good and noble friends who stand by us in times of adversity.

34. July: A Month of Anniversaries

July is not a month that seems to inspire poetic outpourings. Perhaps it is the in-between ordinariness of July, caught between summer-pretty June and summer-glorious August, that fails to stimulate the imagination. I cannot recollect a single poem dedicated to July except for an excruciating one I wrote, as a classroom exercise in my school in Delhi, that began 'In July, month of rain and dust . . .' It is the time of year in North India when the monsoons have just begun and the dust storms of the hot, dry season have not yet cleared away.

But dull, in-between July is a month of momentous anniversaries. There is Bastille Day and American Independence Day and the July Conspiracy against Hitler. In Burma, too, the month is notable for a number of significant events in the modern history of our country. In 1947, on 19 July, six months before Burma was officially declared a sovereign independent nation, my father and several of his colleagues were assassinated while a meeting of the Governor's Executive Council was in session. Four gunmen dressed in jungle-green fatigues and armed with automatic weapons pushed their way into the council chamber and opened fire, wiping out seven councillors who were the foremost leaders of the country, a senior member of the civil service, and a young aide-de-camp. It took just a few minutes to perpetrate the deed that has had an immeasurable effect on the evolution of Burma as an independent nation.

The assassinations had been arranged by a veteran politician, U Saw, who chose the way of violence, rather than the ballot box, as the primary means for achieving political power. He had boycotted the elections of April 1947 in which my father's party, the Anti-Fascist People's Freedom League (AFPFL), had won an overwhelming victory. But although he had neither contested nor gained the mandate of the people, U Saw thought that once he had removed those he saw as his arch rivals, he would be called upon to form a new government. In the event it was U Nu, the most senior member of the AFPFL left alive, who succeeded my father.

Fourteen years after Burma became independent, another event of great historical significance took place in July. On 2 March 1962, the democratically elected government was removed by a military coup and state power passed into the hands of the Revolutionary Council headed by General U Ne Win. The students of Rangoon University, with a strong tradition of political activism dating back to the days of the independence movement, did not respond favourably to the establishment of military rule. As unrest increased in the campus, new university regulations were introduced and in the first week of July, students began peaceful demonstrations to protest against these new regulations. Events took a nasty turn on 7 July when soldiers were ordered to open fire on the students. The exact number and nature of the casualties on that fatal day still remain in dispute; it was officially declared that only sixteen students had been killed, but there are claims that the number of dead was well over one hundred. The tragedy of Rangoon University culminated at dawn the next morning: the Students' Union building, which had been a proving ground for young nationalist politicians who later led the country to independence, was dynamited by order of the authorities and reduced to rubble. Some say the building was full of students, all of whom were killed in the blast.

Twenty-six years after the destruction of the historic Union building, the action of the students of Rangoon University once again led to an event of national importance. As a result of student unrest, the Burma Socialist Programme Party (BSPP), which had dominated the country for a quarter of a century, held an emergency Congress on 23 July 1988. It was the first peal in the death knell of one-party dictatorship. At this Congress, the top leaders of the BSPP resigned and the outgoing Chairman U Ne Win announced it was time to decide whether or not the system should be changed to one that recognized the validity of more than one political party. The refusal of the BSPP to put an end to its authoritarian rule triggered off the nationwide public demonstrations which were the beginning of the movement for democracy.

July is an eventful month for me personally as well. It was on 20 July 1989, that I was placed under house arrest. We received the first intimation of what was about to happen when a neighbour came early in the morning to tell us our road was full of troops. Soon after, U Tin U's son drove over to let us know that his father had been prevented from going out for his usual morning walk. That was the beginning of six years of detention.

And it was on 10 July last year that I was released. When U Aung Shwe, U Kyi Maung, U Tin U and I met that evening we simply decided to pick up where we had left off six years ago, to continue with our work. It remains in my memory as a quiet day, not a momentous one.

35. Mystery Weekend

Once upon a time, I read a biography of Arthur James Balfour of Balfour Declaration fame. The book did not really make the man come alive for me, leaving the impression that he was either too private or too intellectual to come across as a vivid human being; or that the author could not do his subtle personality justice. Nevertheless, I liked what I learned about the 'happy Prime Minister'. I particularly like him for the fact that in spite of the metaphysical dabbling, which troubled some of his political colleagues, he possessed a healthy appreciation for the detective story. He was said to have advised a young man that the best way to get a really good rest was not to go away for the weekend but to shut himself up in the house with a detective story. (Or perhaps he said several detective stories.) In any case it is a piece of advice I consider very sound indeed. Some of the most relaxing weekends I have ever enjoyed were those I spent quietly with a sense of all work to date completed, and an absorbing mystery.

My introduction to the detective story was, very conventionally, through Sherlock Holmes. I was about nine years old when a cousin enthralled me with the story of the Blue Carbuncle. Soon after, I was either given or lent a book about Bugs Bunny's antics involving some Big Red Apples. On reading it I was struck by the inanity of the plot: how could Bugs Bunny's adventures compare with those of a man who could, from a careful examination of a battered old hat, gauge the physical and mental attributes, the financial situation and the matrimonial difficulties of its erstwhile owner? I decided that detectives were much more interesting and entertaining than anthropomorphized animals.

My childhood affection for Sherlock Holmes did not wane even after I learnt to think in terms of whodunits rather than detective stories. The lean, laconic individual of Baker Street can hold his own with the private eyes of the Philip Marlowe genre as well as the intelligent, understated breed of Inspectors Grant and Dalgleish. And the dash of French artist's blood in his veins ('Art in the blood is liable to take the strangest form') makes him more fascinating than the supposedly exotic investigators like Hercule Poirot. But of course it is not the detective or the spy alone who makes a weekend spent with a mystery so satisfactory. Apart from the complexity of the plot and the element of suspense, the style of writing, the little details that build up the atmosphere of the story and the fascination of secondary characters all greatly contribute to my enjoyment of a whodunit.

While Inspector Maigret is a great favourite of mine, Madame Maigret is an even greater favourite. I like best the stories in which she features large and comfortable, always at her cooking pots, always polishing, always mollycoddling her big baby of a husband. Even more than the domestic vignettes of the Maigrets, I enjoy the descriptions of the sights and smells of Paris and the food the gourmand inspector eats with solid appreciation. The small restaurants he discovers in the midst of his investigations seem to specialize in robust, full-flavoured provincial dishes reminiscent of Elizabeth David's French country cooking.

It is probably because of my love of experimenting in the kitchen, a pastime in which I no longer have time to indulge, that the eating habits of fictional characters are of such interest to me. I seem to remember that in one of his adventures, which I read years ago and the title of which I have forgotten, Maigret expressed a dislike for calves' liver; in another, however, he claims that if there is anything he likes better than hot calves' liver *à la bonne femme*, it was the same dish served cold. An inconsistency as intriguing as any of his cases. I cannot recall with any clarity a single plot of any of the stories about Nero Wolfe that I have read but the flavour of the confabulations he has about food with his Swiss chef lingers. And it was because of this obese private investigator's fulsome praise of the chicken fricassee with dumplings he ate at a church fête that I learnt to cook that deliciously homely dish.

Of course one does not read whodunits for memorable descriptions of food. Does George Smiley ever eat? I cannot remember. And one does not recollect, as one follows the developments of espionage in Berlin, that Len Deighton has written a number of cook books. As for Dick Francis, horse feed is more germane than human diet to his plots but that does not make his fast-moving tales any less gripping.

Why is it that English women produce some of the best crime fictions? I am thinking of Dorothy Sayers, Josephine Tey, P. D. James and Ruth Rendell. Theses and probably books have been written on that subject. It is a mystery I would like to have the opportunity to mull over some time when a weekend of leisure reading becomes a possibility. In the meantime, there are enough complexities in Burmese politics to keep one's faculties for unravelling intrigues fully engaged.

36. Communication

Apparently there are actually people who enjoy the unblinking scrutiny of a camera lens and the relentless glare of the flashlights. I am not one of them as I often find it quite exhausting to pose for photographers when there is an insistent piece of work waiting to be completed, or when I am longing for a few quiet minutes with a cup of tea. But with seasoned professionals who have a clear idea of what kind of pictures they would like and how these could best be achieved in prevailing circumstances, the photographic session provides an opportunity for a welcome period of relaxation, time off in the middle of a frantic schedule.

It is good to sit for photographers who are able to explain precisely what they would like you to do but who, at the same time, remain fully aware that you are a human being with muscles that tire and ache when held rigid in positions, not a robot model with a fixed smile. I like best those occasions when I can read peacefully, or prop myself up against a bit of furniture and take a little rest while the camera clicks away unobtrusively.

During a session with two pleasant photographers the other day, I was able to go through almost the whole of *From the Morning of the World*, a slim volume of poems translated from the *Manyoshu*. Sitting on the veranda in the cool stillness of the monsoon afternoon, I savoured again some of my favourite lines. It was refreshing to take a mental rest for a short while from the rate of inflation and, instead, to dwell on images of winter mist hanging low over blue reed beds and wild ducks calling chill, chill, to each other. The description of a flowering orange tree blanching a backyard was a soothing change from an analysis of the yo-yoing of the value of the Burmese currency.

And compared to the latest reports on the harassment of NLD members, a man riding, 'Haggard, on a jet-black horse under the scarlet shine of autumn leaves on Kamunabi', presented a relatively tranquil vision.

A poem by a priest provided enough food for thought to take me through a fair part of the photographic session:

> With what should I compare this world?
> With the white wake left behind
> A ship that dawn watched row away
> Out of its own conceiving mind.[1]

The whole world no more than a mere spume and those busy cameras clicking away trying to capture and preserve on celluloid a transient fleck of existence.

From where does man's passion for recording people and events spring? Did cave dwellers paint hunting scenes to pass an idle hour or was it fulfilment of an unconscious need to immortalize their deeds for posterity? Or was it an attempt to communicate to others their view of life around them, an embryonic form of media activity? What are newspapers, radio, television and other means of mass communication all about? Some who put more emphasis on the mass than on the communication might say cynically that these are simply about making money by catering to the public taste for sensationalism and scandal. But genuine communication constitutes a lot more than mere commerce in news, views and information.

During the year since my release from house arrest I have met hundreds of journalists, both professional and amateur. There are days when I have to give so many interviews in quick succession I feel a little dazed. There are times when I am so tired I am not able to do much more than repeat the same answers to the same questions, feeling very much like a schoolgirl repeating a lesson in class. There have been agonizing sessions when language difficulties make it a struggle for the interviewer and myself to communicate with each other. Then there are those sessions when perception, rather than language, is the problem and questions puzzle while answers are misunderstood and are sometimes misrepresented to the extent that there is little in common between what is said and what appears in print. It all shows that communication between human beings is interesting, frustrating, exhilarating, infuriating, intricate, exhausting – and essential.

Experienced professional journalists can make even the last interview of a gruelling day more of a relaxation than an ordeal. They know how to put the questions so that new facets appear to an old situation and talking to them becomes a learning process. They combine thorough, enquiring minds with an integrity and a human warmth that make conversation with them stimulating and enjoyable. Good photographers and good journalists are masters at communication, with a talent for presenting as accurately as possible what is happening in one part of the world to the rest of the globe. They are a boon to those of us who live in lands where there is not freedom of expression.

1 *From the Morning of the World*, translated by Graeme Wilson, Harvill, London, 1991.

37. Death in Custody (1)

On 2 August, U Hla Than, an NLD Member of Parliament elected in 1990, died in the Rangoon General Hospital as a political prisoner of the SLORC. His constituency, the Coco Islands, is the smallest in the country but one of the best known. The chief of this small group of islands which lie in the Indian Ocean became notorious as a penal settlement for political prisoners after the first military coup of 1958. It was a place where every aspect pleased, vast stretches of ocean, sapphire skies, sandy beaches, graceful swaying palms, and only man seeking to crush and humiliate his fellow man was vile. The penal settlement was dismantled in the late 1960s and there remained on the islands a naval outpost, a skeleton administration and several families who were largely engaged in work connected to the coconut industry. The total population in 1990 was a little over 1000.

U Hla Than and four other members of the NLD set out for greater Coco Island on 4 May 1990, twenty-three days before the elections were scheduled to take place. There they established their headquarters in a small wood and bamboo bungalow and went to work with the will to win support for their cause. House to house canvassing was not permitted, there were strict regulations regarding the distribution of pamphlets and U Hla Than had visited the home of a school teacher a couple of times. He was asked to sign an undertaking not to make any more visits to the house of any civil servant. He refused, explaining that he had merely been paying social calls, not engaging in any electioneering work. Despite the restrictions, the intrepid five carried on with their mission to convey their message of democracy to the people of the islands, long cut adrift from political developments on the mainland.

Although the monsoons had already begun, the morning of 27 May dawned sunny. Nearly 450 of the 613 people on the island above the age of eighteen cast their votes in the two polling stations to choose between U Hla Than and the candidate of the National Union Party, the erstwhile Burma Socialist Programme Party which had ruled the country for twenty-six years. Voting ended around four o'clock in the afternoon and the counting of votes was completed by 7.30 in the evening. The NLD candidate won with 56.94 per cent of the eligible vote. What took place on the Coco Island might have been described as a mini-election but the achievement of U Hla Than and his team was a major one. When they got back to Rangoon they were given a well-deserved heroes' welcome by colleagues and supporters.

At the time he was elected a Member of Parliament, U Hla Than was forty-five years old. He was born to a family of peasant farmers and completed his secondary school education in Moulmein. At the age of twenty, he entered the Burmese navy. A young man of grit and industry who believed in the value of education, he continued with his studies during his years of service and passed the matriculation examination in 1975. He retired from the navy in 1977 and went on to study law. In 1980 he gained the LL.B. from the University of Rangoon.

U Hla Than took an active part in the democracy movement of 1988 as member of the Rangoon Lawyers' Association. Later he joined the NLD and became the Party Committee Chairman of one of the important townships of the Rangoon Division. When preparations for the elections began, he offered to stand as the party candidate in the Coco Islands, a constituency that aroused little enthusiasm. His offer was gratefully accepted.

The official announcements of the results of the elections were dragged out over weeks but it was widely known within a matter of days that the NLD had won a spectacular victory. The country was in a jubilant mood, proud of the outcome of the first democratic elections in three decades, full of hope for the future, confident that at last there would be a government that would be transparent and accountable and which would gain trust and respect both at home and abroad. Few in Burma suspected then that they were going to be the victims of one of the most blatant acts of deceit practised on any people. Few realized then that the fair promises of a democratic transfer of power were worth less than the withered palm leaves drifting off the shores of the Coco Islands.

It was some two months after the elections, when SLORC still showed no signs of relinquishing power, or of convening Parliament, that a climate of unease began to set in. And when U Kyi Maung and other key members of the NLD were taken into custody in September, the unease turned into dismay and disillusionment. The next month, a number of Members of Parliament, including U Hla Than, were arrested. In April 1991 U Hla Than was tried by a martial law court, accused of complicity in attempts to set up a parallel government and sentenced to twenty-five years' imprisonment for high treason. Now, five years later, he is dead, a victim of a warped process of law and a barbaric penal system.

38. Death in Custody (2)

The death certificate of U Hla Than, NLD Member of Parliament for the Coco Islands who died on 2 August as a political prisoner of the present military regime of Burma, stated that he had died of 'extensive Koch's lung [tuberculosis] and HIV infection'. Coincidentally on the day of his death, extracts from a report on conditions in Burmese prisons by a student activist who had served time in the infamous Insein Jail, where U Hla Than was incarcerated for nearly six years, appeared in the *Nation* newspaper of Bangkok. The report states that owing to drug abuse 'there is ... a high prevalence of HIV/Aids in prisons. When administering injections, the doctors only give half or less than half of the phial to one patient, giving the rest to another patient from the same needle and syringe, almost guaranteeing that any blood-carried infections will spread.' There can be little doubt that U Hla Than's death was brought about by the abysmal prison conditions that do not bear scrutiny by independent observers. The Red Cross left Burma in 1995 because of the refusal of the authorities to allow inspection of the prisons of the country.

U Hla Than is certainly not the first prisoner of conscience to have died in the custody of SLORC. Some leading members of the NLD can be counted among those who have given their lives for the right to adhere to their deeply held political principles. The first of those was U Maung Ko who, ironically, died during the visit of Mrs Sadako Ogata, who had been sent by the United Nations Human Rights Commission to make enquiries into the human rights situation in Burma. U Maung Ko, fifty-two at the time of his death, was a civil servant who worked in the Rangoon Port Commissioner's Office before he entered the democracy movement in 1988 as the General

Secretary of the Dock Workers' Union. When the NLD was founded he became one of the pioneer members of the party.

U Maung Ko was arrested and taken to Insein Jail during the crackdown on democracy activists in October 1990. In less than three weeks, on 9 November, he was dead. His family learned of his death from workers at the Rangoon General Hospital, where his body was sent from Insein Jail. The authorities claimed U Maung Ko had taken his own life after making a confession of his activities; neither the content of the confession nor the circumstances under which it was extracted have ever been revealed. Many question the verdict of suicide. Friends and members of the family who saw U Maung Ko's body before burial assert that there were many marks on it to indicate that he had been badly tortured.

The next NLD victim among the political prisoners of SLORC was U Ba Thaw, better known as the writer Maung Thaw Ka. *Hsaya* (teacher) Maung Thaw Ka, as he was affectionately addressed by friends, colleagues and admirers, was an unforgettable character. He served in the Burmese navy for many years and was involved in a shipwreck in 1956 while serving as the commanding officer on a coastguard cutter patrolling the south-eastern coastline. When his vessel foundered, Lt. Ba Thaw and the 26 other navy personnel on board transferred to two inflatable life-rafts. One life-raft was lost with all nine passengers on board but the second life-raft was rescued by a Japanese ship twelve days later. By then, seven of the eighteen men on the life-raft were dead and another man died on the rescue ship. Maung Thaw Ka wrote a gripping book about the harrowing time he and his mates spent under a searing sun on the small life-raft, which carried only boiled sweets and water sufficient to keep ten men alive for three days.

Hsaya Maung Thaw Ka's irrepressible sense of humour came across in many of his writings, which could perhaps be described as satire without malice. One of his witticisms became highly popular during the years of socialist rule in Burma. On being told that a fellow writer believed in ghosts, *Hsaya* Maung Thaw Ka riposted: 'He believes in anything, he even believes in the Burma Socialist Programme Party!'

Hsaya Maung Thaw Ka was also a poet. He not only wrote his own poetry, he translated many poems from English into Burmese, some of which were surprisingly romantic: the love poetry of Shakespeare, Robert Herrick, John Donne and Shelley. There was also a translation of William Cowper's 'The Solitude of Alexander Selkirk', which he said was dedicated to himself. Perhaps it was the last verse that appealed to him:

> But the seafowl is gone to her nest,
> The beast is laid down in his lair:
> Even here is a season of rest,
> And I to my cabin repair.
> There is mercy in every place, And mercy,
>   encouraging thought!
> Gives affliction a grace
> And reconciles man to his lot.

But there was no mercy for *Hsaya* Maung Thaw Ka in Insein Jail.

39. Death in Custody (3)

Hsaya Maung Thaw Ka was arrested in 1989 and sentenced by a martial law court to twenty years' imprisonment in October of that year. The SLORC had accused him of seeking to cause an insurrection within the armed forces. At the time he entered Insein Jail, *Hsaya* Maung Thaw Ka was already suffering from a chronic disease that was laying his muscles to waste. His movements were stiff and jerky, and everyday matters, such as bathing, dressing or eating, involved for him a series of difficult manoeuvres which could barely be completed without assistance. For a man with his health problems, life in solitary confinement was a continuous struggle to cope. And *Hsaya* Maung Thaw Ka struggled manfully. But his already much-eroded physical system was unable to withstand the inhuman conditions of Insein Jail for long. In June 1991, *Hsaya* Maung Thaw Ka, navy officer and humorist, poet and political activist, died in custody at the age of sixty-five.

Even during his darkest days in prison, *Hsaya* Maung Thaw Ka's muse did not desert him. In secret he composed poems about the gross injustices committed under military dictatorship with a biting anger entirely removed from his delicate rendering of old English sonnets. 'Twenty years, they say . . . in accordance with that (legal) section of all things that is unclean and despicable,' he wrote with contempt of the sentence which, for him, turned out to be one of death.

October and November of 1990 were months when the SLORC carried out a major crackdown against the movement for democracy. It was in these months that numbers of National League for Democracy Members of Parliament were brought into Insein Jail. Among these men, elected by the people of Burma to form a democratic government but condemned by the military regime to imprisonment, was U Tin Maung Win of Khayan. He had been a prominent student leader in the late 1950s and early 1960s. In 1962, when students protested against the high-handed actions of the military government that had newly come into power, he was the Chairman of the Committee for the Protection of Students' Rights. The next year, as the leader of the Rangoon University Students' Union, he was placed under arrest.

U Tin Maung Win was kept in prison for seven years. But neither that experience, nor the even more deadening one of a quarter of a century of life under the Burmese Way to Socialism, succeeded in killing his political convictions. In 1988, U Tin Maung Win took part in the movement for democracy in concert with the other former student leaders. In the elections of 1990, he contested as the NLD's candidate in his native Khayan against his own brother who represented the National Unity Party, the main adversary of the democratic parties. Five months after his victory in the elections he was arrested.

U Tin Maung Win spent a month at Ye-kyi-ain, an infamous military intelligence interrogation centre, before he was sent to Insein Jail. When he was charged with high treason in January 1991, he was not able to be present at his trial because he was too ill. By 18 January, U Tin Maung Win was dead. The authorities claimed that he had died of leukaemia but before he was incarcerated just four months previously there had been no sign that he was suffering from such a grave disease. It is the contention of those who saw his body that he died as a result of ill treatment in prison.

Last year, U Kyi Saung, secretary of the NLD branch in Myaung-mya, a town in the Irrawaddy division, was arrested. He had attended a Karen New Year ceremony in a Karen village and, there, he had read out the NLD's New Year message of goodwill. This peaceful, innocuous act of courtesy was reported by the Union Solidarity and Development Association, the 'social welfare' organization formed under the aegis of government, to the Myaungmya Township Law and Order Restoration Council and to the local military intelligence unit. The SLORC thereby arrested U Kyi Saung under Section 5 of the 1950 Emergency Act which has come to be known as the 'Can't Stand your Looks' section as it is used indiscriminately against those whom the authorities cannot abide. An elderly man, U Kyi Saung's health deteriorated rapidly and he died in May 1996 before his trial was completed.

I have written only about well-known members of the NLD who died in custody but they are not the only victims of authoritarian injustice. Prisoners of conscience who lost their lives during the 1990s represent a broad range of the Burmese political spectrum and even include a Buddhist monk. Of those sacrificed to the misrule of law, the oldest was seventy-year-old Boh Set Yaung, a member of the Patriotic Old Comrades' League, and the youngest was a nineteen-year-old member of the NLD. The exact number of deaths in custody cannot be ascertained but it is not small and it is rising all the time. The price of liberty has never been cheap and in Burma it is particularly high.

40. Teachers

Vassa, the rainy season retreat, has begun. It is a time for offering robes to monks and for making special efforts towards gaining a better understanding of Buddhist values. In Burma we look upon members of the *sangha* (the Buddhist religious order) as teachers who will lead us along the Noble Eightfold Path. Good teachers do not merely give scholarly sermons, they show us how we should conduct our daily lives in accordance with right understanding, right thought, right speech, right action, right livelihood, right effort, right mindfulness and right concentration.

Not long before my house arrest in 1989, I was granted an audience with the venerable U Pandita, an exceptional teacher in the best tradition of great spiritual mentors whose words act constantly as an aid to a better existence. *Hsayadaw* (holy teacher) U Pandita spoke of the importance of *samma-vaca* or right speech. Not only should one speak only the truth, one's speech should lead to harmony among beings, it should be kind and pleasant and it should be beneficial. One should follow the example of the Lord Buddha who only spoke words that were truthful and beneficial even if at times such speech was not always pleasing to the listener.

The *Hsayadaw* also urged me to cultivate *sati*, mindfulness. Of the five spiritual faculties, *saddha* (faith), *viriya* (energy), *samadhi* (concentration) and *panna* (wisdom), it is only *sati* that can never be in excess. Excessive faith without sufficient wisdom leads to blind faith, while excessive wisdom without sufficient faith leads to undesirable cunning. Too much energy combined with weak concentration leads to restlessness while strong concentration without sufficient energy leads to indolence. But as for *sati*, one can never have too much of it, it is 'never in excess, but always in deficiency'. The truth and value of this Buddhist concept that *Hsayadaw* U Pandita took such pains to impress on me became evident during my years of house arrest.

Like many of my Buddhist colleagues, I decided to put my time under detention to good use by practising meditation. It was not an easy process. I did not have a teacher and my early attempts were more than a little frustrating. There were days when I found my failure to discipline my mind in accordance with prescribed meditation practices so infuriating I felt I was doing myself more harm than good. I think I would have given up but for the advice of a famous Buddhist teacher, that whether or not one wanted to practise meditation, one should do so for one's own good. So I gritted my teeth and kept at it, often rather glumly. Then my husband gave me a copy of *Hsayadaw* U Pandita's book, *In This Very Life: The Liberation Teachings of the Buddha*. By studying this book carefully, I learnt how to overcome the difficulties of meditation and to realize its benefits. I learnt how practising meditation led to increased mindfulness in everyday life, and again and again I recalled the *Hsayadaw*'s words on the importance of *sati* with appreciation and gratitude.

In my political work I have been helped and strengthened by the teachings of members of the *sangha*. During my very first campaign trip across Burma, I received invaluable advice from monks in different parts of the country. In Prome a *Hsayadaw* told me to keep in mind the hermit Sumedha, who sacrificed the possibility of early liberation for himself alone and underwent many lives of striving that he might save others from suffering. So must you be prepared to strive for as long as might be necessary to achieve good and justice, exhorted the venerable *Hsayadaw*.

In a monastery at Pakokku, the advice that an abbot gave to my father when he came to that town more than forty years ago was repeated to me: 'Do not be frightened every time there is an attempt to frighten you, but do not be entirely without fear. Do not become elated every time you are praised, but do not be entirely lacking in elation.' In other words, while maintaining courage and humility, one should not abandon caution and healthy self-respect.

When I visited Natmauk, my father's home town, I went to the monastery where he studied as a boy. There the abbot gave a sermon on the four causes of decline and decay: failure to recover that which has been lost, omitting to repair that which has been damaged; disregard of the need for reasonable economy; and the elevation to leadership of those without morality or learning. The abbot went on to explain how these traditional Buddhist views should be interpreted to help us build a just and prosperous society in the modern age.

Of the words of wisdom I gathered during that journey across central Burma, those of a ninety-one-year-old *Hsayadaw* of Sagaing are particularly memorable. He sketched out for me tersely how it would be to work for democracy in Burma. 'You will be attacked and reviled for engaging in honest politics,' pronounced the *Hsayadaw*, 'but you must persevere. Lay down an investment in *dukkha* [suffering] and you will gain *sukha* [bliss].'

41. Some Problems of Definition

There is an expression much bandied about these days which, in its Burmanized form, sounds very much like 'jeans shirt'. This has nothing to do with the denim mania that has come to Burma together with foreign beers and cigarettes, walking shoes, expensive batiks, Pajero cars and all the other paraphernalia so dear to the hearts of the small, privileged élite who have profited wonderfully from the selectively open market economy. The expression actually refers to 'Gene Sharp', the author of some works on 'political defiance'. These writings seem to be exercising the authorities in Burma considerably. Last month, nineteen political prisoners were tried in Mandalay and they were all sentenced to seven years' imprisonment each on a charge of high treason. The possession of copies of books by Gene Sharp seemed to have been taken as part of the evidence against the defendants. (Not that 'defendant' is an appropriate word to use in connection with political detainees in Burma as they have no real right of defence at all.)

At a government press conference this month, more references were made to political defiance. When a correspondent asked whether these political defiance courses initiated by Gene Sharp trained people to commit political assassinations and other acts of violence, a spokesman for SLORC said they did not know, as they had not attended any of those courses. It is very puzzling that courses, the contents of which the authorities are totally ignorant of, should be seen as treasonable. It was also alleged at the press conference that I had talked about political defiance with an American visitor. When a correspondent asked me whether this was so, I said it was not so, as I could not at all recall any conversation about Gene Sharp or his books or the courses in political defiance he is said to have conducted. Later, it occurred to me that both my interviewer and I had merely been thinking of political defiance in terms of SLORC-speak. In fact, political defiance is no more synonymous with Gene Sharp than with denim shirts. It can be defined simply as the natural response of anybody who disagrees with the opinions of the government in power. In that sense, the great majority of people in Burma are perpetually engaged in political defiance in their hearts, if not in their actions.

Another interesting question posed by a correspondent at the SLORC press conference was why the authorities objected to the opposition carrying out its work. The answer was that it was dangerous. A government that has promised a transfer to 'multi-party democracy' views the work of the opposition as *dangerous*? A self-proclaimed conservationist might as well chop down trees indiscriminately and massacre rare, and not so rare, species with wild abandon.

There are two problems of definition in the above paragraph. This repeated reference to 'multi-party democracy' since the SLORC took over power. Surely the expression is a tautology? And 'one-party democracy' would be oxymoronic. Democracy basically means choice and political choice means the existence of more than one effective political party or force. 'Democracy' by itself should be sufficient to indicate a pluralistic political approach.

Then there is the question of the word 'opposition'. The NLD is often referred to as 'the opposition'. But it was the NLD that won the only democratic elections held in more than thirty years: and won it with an overwhelming majority such as was not achieved by any other political party in those countries that made the transition from dictatorship to democracy in the 1980s and 1990s. The word 'opposition' when applied to a party which won the unequivocal mandate of the people takes on a peculiar ring. But leaving that aside, how does one define the work of an opposition in any country which claims to be heading towards (multi-party) democracy?

A group guided by the political legacy of a prominent communist leader who engaged in armed rebellion against the government for several decades after Burma regained her independence, and who later laid down arms and recanted, came to see me some months ago. They read out the political guidelines laid down by their late leader which, among other things, condemned the idea of any work aimed at removing a government in power. I explained to them that this was unacceptable to anybody who truly believed in democracy. In a genuine democracy, it is the legitimate function of opposition parties to work at removing the government through the democratic process. Any political ideology that disallows parties from carrying out opposition activities and presenting themselves to the country as viable alternatives to the existing government cannot be said to have anything to do with democracy. To view opposition as dangerous is to misunderstand the basic concepts of democracy. To oppress the opposition is to assault the very foundation of democracy.

42. Misrule of Law

As I understand it, a kangaroo court is so called because it is a burlesque performance where the process of the law takes heart-stopping leaps and bounds. Out of curiosity, I looked up the entry on kangaroos in the *Encyclopaedia Britannica* to see how far these marsupial mammals can clear in a leap. Apparently the record is 13.5 metres. This is far superior to the Olympic long-jump record. It is no surprise then that the erratic course of justice in a kangaroo court is outside the bounds of normal human conduct.

I have written about the challenges that political dissidents in Burma have to face. Everybody committed to taking an active part in the endeavour to return the country to democracy has to be prepared to go to prison at any time. It usually happens in the middle of the night, appropriately, as there can be fewer deeds more akin to darkness than that of depriving innocent people of a normal, healthy life. The ones most vulnerable to arrest are members of the NLD. Many of them are already seasoned jail veterans who, at casual moments, exchange prison yarns and instruct the as yet uninitiated on such matters as the kind of treatment they can expect at the interrogation sessions and what they should take with them when the banging on the door comes: a change of clothing, soap, toothpaste and toothbrush, medicines, a blanket or two, et cetera, all in a plastic bag. Nothing so respectable as a knapsack or suitcase is permitted. And do not be fooled if the people who turn up at the door, usually without a warrant, say that they will only be keeping you for a few days. That could well translate into a twenty-year sentence.

When U Win Htein, a key member of my office staff, was arrested one night last May, he had a bag ready packed. He had previously spent six years in Insein Jail: he was one of the people taken away from my house in 1989 on the day I was detained and he was released only in February 1995. When U Win Htein asked those who had come to take him away whether they had an arrest warrant, they replied that it was not necessary as charges had already been moved against him and his sentence had been decided. So much for the concept of the law that deems a person innocent until proven guilty.

Section 340 (1) of the Code of Criminal Procedure provides that 'any person accused of an offence before a criminal court, or against whom proceedings are instituted under this code, in any such court, may of right be defended by a pleader.' This basic right to counsel is systematically denied to political prisoners in Burma. They are not even allowed to make contact with their families. The authorities generally refuse to give any information on detainees who have not yet been tried. The NLD and the families of political prisoners have to make strenuous enquiries to find out where they are, with what 'crime' they are to be charged and when and where the trials would take place. Usually the trials of political prisoners are conducted in a special courthouse within the jail precincts.

Last month a number of political prisoners were tried in Insein Jail. When the NLD heard that U Win Htein and some others were going to be produced at court on a certain day, a lawyer was sent to defend them. The Special Branch officer at the jail questioned by the lawyer said he did not know anything about a trial. But the trial took place while the lawyer was waiting at the gate and continued after he left in the afternoon. The next week, a number of lawyers again went to Insein Jail, accompanied by the families of the prisoners, on the day they had heard the trial was to continue. This time they managed to get into the prison courthouse. However, they were only allowed to cross-examine four of the twenty-four witnesses for the prosecution.

The next morning, the lawyers and the families of the prisoners arrived at Insein Jail at nine o'clock, as they had heard sentence would be passed that day. The area around the jail entrance was full of security personnel and all the shops along the road were shut. The lawyers were refused entry. They were told sentence would only be passed at the end of the month and were asked to leave. However, as the magistrate concerned with the case had been seen at the Insein Township Magistrate's Court, the lawyers were convinced the trial was scheduled to proceed within a matter of hours and continued to wait outside the jail. The magistrate eventually arrived and entered the prison precincts at around two o'clock and came out again after about forty minutes. The lawyers followed him to the Insein Township Court to ask what kind of sentence had been passed. The magistrate, very nervous and surrounded by security personnel, would only say that an application should be made to copy the records of the court proceedings. Some days later the government media announced that U Win Htein and others had been given seven-year prison sentences each.

The sight of kangaroos bounding away across an open prairie can sometimes be rather beautiful. The spectacle of the process of law bounding away from accepted norms of justice is very ugly at all times.

43. Uncivil Service (1)

Visitors to Burma seldom have much notion of the complexities of everyday life in our country. On the surface, things appear smooth and serene and it is only those who are familiar with states ruled by inefficient dictatorial regimes who are able to see what is really going on.

Take a taxi through the streets of Rangoon and observe the cars going by: almost all of these vehicles are running on black market petrol. The price of petrol sold at government pumping stations is 25 kyats a gallon. However, as no car is entitled to more than four gallons a week (some are entitled to less) of this official issue, people are forced to resort to additional sources of supply. This black market petrol has gone up in price within the last month from 180 kyats to 350 kyats a gallon and most of it is leaked out from government departments.

There is more to running a car than finding a good source of petrol. Car licences have to be renewed annually. Owners have to ask the Department of Road Transport Administration for a date on which their vehicles can be inspected and passed as roadworthy. If you do not want to go through the rigmarole of making an appointment in advance, you pay a certain sum of money to have your car checked immediately. Then you go on to bribe the person assigned to check your vehicle. Otherwise, you will be sent back to change the lights, or to repaint the chassis, or to replace some part of the engine. People have been sent away as many as four or five times to undertake repairs 'necessary' to make the vehicle roadworthy until they saw the light and produced several hundred kyats. It is no use complaining or getting angry: the employees in the Department of Road Transport Administration have to make ends meet.

Making ends meet is the overriding preoccupation of civil servants in Burma. Their pay is ridiculously low. A Director-General, the highest ranking civil servant, earns an official monthly salary of 2500 kyats a month, the equivalent of about $15. This is not even enough to feed a family of four, modestly, for a week. Consequently civil servants have to find ways and means of earning extra income.

There are those who would say that Burmese people are resourceful by nature. It is more likely the case that all peoples who have to live under a system where following the straight and narrow path too often leads to impecuniosity learn to be resourceful. And in such situations, 'resourceful' is often simply a euphemism for 'dishonest' or 'corrupt'. If you happen to work in the electricity department in Burma you quickly learn that you can supplement your income by making deals with householders who do not wish to pay their electricity bills in full. And you soon find out that you can squeeze a regular, tidy sum from the entrepreneurs of businesses, such as ice-making, for whom an electricity cut would be catastrophic. A lineman can make a supplementary income amounting to thousands of kyats a month if he happens to be fortunate enough to be in charge of an area where a number of vulnerable enterprises are situated.

If you work in the telecommunications department too, you put your 'resourcefulness' to quick use. When a telephone fails to work, the owner has to appeal for repairs. And the most effective appeals are those of a solid pecuniary nature. As in the electricity department, the pay-up-or-be-cut tactic can assure a regular source of supplementary income. The long waiting list for telephones also provides employees in the telecommunications department with opportunities for exercising their ingenuity. They can 'co-operate' in the transfer of already connected telephones to different owners, or they can expedite the connection of a new telephone. All, of course, for a certain consideration, which could amount to a five figure sum.

The Inland Revenue Department, as might be expected, is a section of the civil service where employees can earn sums 'on the side' many times larger than their regular salaries. The best customers of this department are businessmen who have no inhibitions about evading taxes. But that does not mean honest businessmen who wish to declare their incomes correctly are safe from the resourcefulness (or rapacity, if you wish) of the personnel of the department. Their taxable income is arbitrarily assessed at a rate far higher than the correct one until they decide that honesty is not, after all, the best policy in dealing with such matters and agree to co-operate with the officials concerned.

The corruption of the civil services is not just an urban phenomenon. Farmers have to sell a quota of their harvest to the government at stipulated prices well below the market rate. The state employees who weigh the grain at rice depots manage to put aside a substantial amount of rice for themselves. This rice they sell at the market price to those farmers who have had bad harvests, so they can produce the necessary government quota for which, of course, the poor farmers are paid only the state price. It is no wonder that in Burma civil servants are generally viewed as public predators rather than public benefactors.

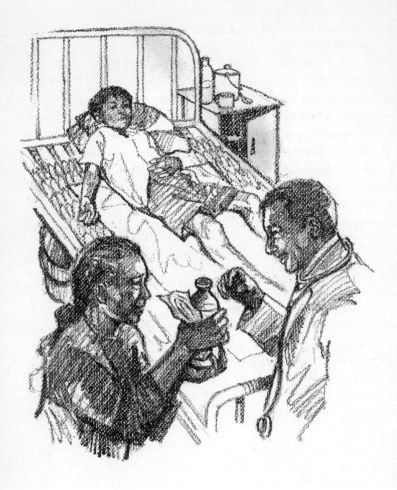

44. Uncivil Service (2)

On my release from house arrest last year, people gathered outside the gates of my home to greet me and to demonstrate their support for the movement for democracy. It was the monsoon season and the crowds would stand and wait in the dripping rain until I went out to speak to them. This continued day after day for more than a month, then I negotiated with our supporters an arrangement which was more convenient for all concerned: we would meet regularly at four o'clock on Saturdays and Sundays. Thus were born the public rallies that have been taking place outside my house every weekend.

A few months after the weekend rallies had become established as a regular political feature, I invited the audience to write to me about matters they would like me to discuss. The response was immediate and enthusiastic. Letters on a wide range of subjects, political, economic, social and religious, were put into the mail-box we hung outside the gate for that purpose. A recurring theme in these letters, which continue to come in, is the widespread corruption among civil servants, in particular in the sectors of health and education.

In Burma health care is ostensibly provided free of charge by the state. But in recent years, the contributions expected from the community have risen to such an extent that it is no longer possible to think of health care as 'free'. By 'contributions' I do not mean just monetary donations made by the public towards health care projects, although such donations are not inconsiderable. I am referring to the fact that government health care facilities now provide merely services while patients have to provide almost everything else: medicines, cotton wool, surgical spirit, bandages and even equipment necessary for surgery.

Patients not only have to make their own arrangements for getting the necessary medical supplies, they also have to bribe the hospital staff in order to receive satisfactory service. It is not just doctors and nurses who have to be sweetened with gifts, hospital orderlies also have to be paid if one's time as an invalid is to be passably comfortable. Apparently it is common practice for orderlies to neglect their cleaning duties unless duly compensated. And they are also said to give patients who have to be wheeled from one part of the hospital to another a rough ride until a requisite sum of money has changed hands. Then there are the doorkeepers and other administrative staff whose hands have to be greased to smooth the path of family members who need to go in and out at all hours to deliver necessary supplies.

While nothing can excuse callousness in those who should be giving succour to the ill and dying, it cannot be ignored that the deterioration in state health care is largely the result of maladministration. High motivation cannot be expected of grossly underpaid staff working with poorly maintained equipment in dilapidated, unhygienic surroundings.

In recent years, the emergence of a private sector has made health care at expensive clinics and nursing homes available to those who are well off. There are indications that among those who cannot afford private health care, that is to say, the large majority of the population, there is an increasing tendency to rely on folk or traditional medicine rather than place themselves at the mercy of the state health care system.

Even more than letters about the unsavoury conditions in our hospitals, I receive letters about the disgraceful state of our education system. Education, like health care, is ostensibly free in Burma but again, as with health care, the contribution exacted from the community is getting higher by the day.

Inadequate school funds are supplemented by 'donations' collected for various purposes: sports day, new buildings, school furniture, teacher–parent association fund, religious festivals. Underpaid teachers supplement their incomes by giving tuition outside school hours. The fees range from 1000 kyats to 10 000 kyats for each pupil, depending on the grade in which they are studying and the number of subjects in which they are coached. The poor quality of teaching in the schools forces all parents who can afford the fees to send their children to such tuition classes.

Examinations provide teachers as well as employees of the education department with opportunities for lucrative business. Examination questions, advance information on grades achieved and the marking up of low grades can all be obtained at a price.

There was a time when civil servants in our country were seen as an élite corps: well-educated, well-trained and well-paid, capable of giving good service to the community. Now they are generally regarded with fear and revulsion or with pity. State employees who have not become part of the syndrome of daily corruption, either from principle or from lack of opportunity, are unable to maintain an appropriate standard of living. They are the nouveau poor of Burma.

45. Strange Siege

As I have remarked often enough, life is certainly not dull for dissidents in Burma. But sometimes a little bit of dullness does not come amiss. In fact it provides a measure of welcome relief, time in which to stand and stare for at least a few minutes a day.

The NLD decided to hold an All Burma Party Congress on the eighth anniversary of the day when it was founded, on 27 September. Now one might have thought that such an event, which is part of the normal routine of any political party, would not have caused the authorities to do more than perhaps cock an inquisitive eyebrow and set the Military Intelligence running around busily gathering information. One would not have imagined that they would be rocked to the very soles of their military boots. Well, one would have been wrong.

On the evening of 26 September, we received information that once again, as at the time of our proposed conference for NLD Members of Parliament in May, the authorities were rounding up those who were to attend the Congress. Around 9.30 p.m. army trucks started going past my house and later, a police car or two went along the already cleared street with sirens blaring. It was all rather tedious and we went to sleep. When I awoke at 5 a.m., the unusual silence told me that our road had been blocked off. It was not altogether a surprise.

At 8 a.m., U Tin U, one of our Deputy Chairmen, was let through and he told us what had been going on outside. Our helpers who had been scheduled to arrive at 4 a.m. to start cooking the meal that we would be offering to monks as a prelude to our Congress had been prevented from entering the street. After some negotiation, two of our NLD women members were allowed in to take charge of the huge pots of curry that had already been half-prepared the night before. Soon after, our Chairman U Aung Shwe and our other Deputy Chairman U Kyi Maung also arrived.

I learnt that a number of NLD members who had come for the Congress were at the road junction not far from my house where barricades had been placed to prevent people from entering the street. At about ten o'clock we decided to walk over to them and tell them to go to the NLD headquarters. Walking along a street deserted except for security troops was not a new experience for me. This had happened again and again during my campaign trips around Burma in 1988 and 1989. And last April too, on Burmese New Year's day, we had walked down our street when it was emptied of everybody except security personnel and members of the Union Solidarity and Development Association (USDA) armed with surreptitious batons, with which they had been instructed to beat any members of the NLD who penetrated the barricades.

The USDA were also present this time, a couple of busloads of them milling around in the public garden at the top of the road for a purpose that we found hard to discern. When we reached the road junction our party members, who had been made to go to the other side of the street, came over to ask us what we wanted them to do. We told them to go to our headquarters and were just about to go back home ourselves when an army officer came to ask us to disperse. It was a typical over-reaction, unnecessary and quite senseless as the crowd around us was made up largely of security personnel, uniformed as well as in plain clothes.

That afternoon, after the religious ceremony to commemorate the founding of the NLD had been completed, U Aung Shwe and I went out to see how things were at the party headquarters. We found that the road where the building was situated had also been closed off. That very evening, the landlord was illegally forced to annul the lease and to remove the NLD signboard from the building. The authorities had obviously decided to take all possible steps to prevent us from carrying out the legitimate work of a normal political party.

Now nearly a week after the 27th, the road to my house continues to be blocked off. But U Aung Shwe, U Kyi Maung and U Tin U come over every day and we carry on with our work. 'It is always still at the centre of the storm,' U Tin U remarked. And certainly there has been a great calm in my house even as the authorities have been arresting hundreds of our supporters, making wild accusations against us and trying to force the landlords of our party offices to remove NLD signboards.

There is the proverbial silver lining to these storm clouds of increased official repression. The state of semi-siege provides me with an opportunity to take a rest from the gruelling timetable that I normally follow. I do not have to rush through my meals, and I have even been able to spare an hour a day for walking round and round the garden: a wonderfully relaxing and invigorating form of exercise which I have not been able to indulge in for years. This strange interlude should serve to make me fighting fit for whatever challenges we may have to face in the future.

46. Sequel to the Siege

Things tend to happen in the middle of the night in military-ruled Burma. That is the time when houses are checked by the local authorities for unreported visitors; that is the time when dissidents are hauled off to interrogation centres; that was the time when the road to my house was blocked off before our Party Congress planned for 27 September. That was also the time the barricades were removed after eleven quiet days during which my house had remained cut off from the outside world, although I myself was free to come and go.

Taking the rare opportunity of completing my work at a reasonable hour, I had gone to bed at eleven o'clock on the night of 7 October. Around midnight I became aware of voices in the garden. I assumed that some of the thirty-one guests besieged in my house were having a late-night discussion. But as the voices continued for some time in increasingly animated tones I began to think that there had been some kind of incident. I was wondering if I should find out what was going on when the voices faded away. However just as I was about to drift off to sleep, the voices started up again, louder than ever. Eventually at 2 a.m. I went down to investigate and discovered that the road had been opened up again.

The next morning, visitors started arriving: there were our party members who had just been released from detention, there were well-wishers and supporters and there were journalists. A press conference had to be arranged at short notice. We were back to the normal, hectic routine. Within a few hours, the deliciously slow pace of the past eleven days was but a wistful memory. Eleven days is not a long time but it is long enough to make one appreciate a different tempo of life.

We had four normal days, four days in which to assess the events of the past fortnight and to make arrangements for the work of the party to proceed. A question that came up frequently was whether we intended to continue with our weekend rallies. My reply was that we would continue for as long as the people were prepared to come. The authorities must have realized that the people *were* prepared to continue their support of our rallies, because at midnight on Friday, 11 October, the sound of police sirens and rumbling trucks with which we had become familiar announced that access to my house had once again been cut off.

There was a slightly *déjà vu* air about the next morning. We all smiled at each other and wondered how long we would be cut off this time. However there were a number of circumstances that differed from the last time that the road was closed. To begin with, we did not have to worry about what to do with huge quantities of half-cooked food, which was a relief. Secondly, U Tin U did not appear. I have written several times about our Deputy Chairman U Tin U, one time Commander-in-Chief of the armed forces of Burma, but I have not had occasion to mention a particularly lovable trait of his: he has the strongly developed protective instinct of the truly honourable soldier. Whenever a difficult situation arises he arrives to offer his protection and assistance. When he did not arrive I knew that he must have been prevented from coming. I waited until about 11 a.m., then went to U Kyi Maung's house to find out what was going on.

A number of people were gathered at U Kyi Maung's house. Among them were some NLD Members of Parliament from outside Rangoon. Their bright expressions and high spirits warmed my heart. These were men who hold sacred the promises they made to their electorate six years ago, who have faced many hardships and who are prepared to face many more that they may keep faith with those who put their trust in them. It is people like them who make all sacrifices seem worthwhile; it is as much for love of them as for love of freedom and justice that I am engaged in the struggle for democracy.

At U Kyi Maung's house, my suspicion that this time, none of our *lugyis* (elders) would be allowed to come to my house was confirmed. It just meant that I would have to come out to see them, to confer with them and to carry on the work of the party. 'Business as usual' was our motto although we had to be somewhat unorthodox in our methods. For the next few days we met at different houses at different times to complete work that should have been conducted in a regular party conference. Everywhere we went, the authorities exhibited the most intense, not to say vulgar, curiosity, surrounding the places with Military Intelligence and security personnel, wasting a lot of video and camera film recording all the comings and goings.

We estimate that the government intelligence organizations must spend from 80 to 90 per cent of their time, energy and money on matters related to NLD activities. How much more sensible it would be to come to a civilized settlement that would remove the need for spies and sieges.

47. Continuum

This is getting absurd. The road to my house keeps being blocked and unblocked and then blocked again with the agitated rhythm of a demented yo-yo. Let us recapitulate the events of the last month. The first time the barricades went up was at midnight on 26 September. Eleven days later, at midnight on 7 October, the barricades were removed. Then at midnight on 11 October, the road was blocked off again.

This second blockade lasted until 4.30 p.m. on 21 October. But later that night, around 9.30 p.m., the road was blocked off again. 'Possibly there is some method in their madness' was all I could think as I went off to sleep. The next morning I discovered that the road had been unblocked at three o'clock in the early morning. That day, 22 October, was a normal working day: well, more or less normal by NLD standards, with people coming over to exchange notes on how they had been chased and beaten by security personnel, how they had been taken into detention and how they had been released. At midnight that very day the road was blocked off yet once more.

There are slight variations from one blockade to the other. The first time I was free to come and go, and key members of the NLD Executive Committee were allowed to come to my house. The second time, I was still free to come and go but others were not allowed in except on 19 October, when I made my usual monthly offering to monks in remembrance of my father. U Aung Shwe, our NLD Chairman, and our two Deputy Chairmen, U Kyi Maung and U Tin U, and their wives were able to join us for the ceremony.

The second blockade was a busy time for us as a number of party meetings had to be conducted at various venues. It was on the day we finished our fourth meeting that the road was opened again at the unexpected time of 4.30 in the afternoon.

The third blockade which started at midnight on 22 October found us quite blasé. The next morning, a Wednesday, I got ready to go out to see where we should hold the meeting that had been scheduled to take place at my house. But just as I was about to leave, the military intelligence officer in charge of security in my house came to convey a 'request' to the effect that I should not go out that day. A civil request deserves a civil response, so I said that would be all right provided those who had to attend the meeting were allowed to come to my house. This was arranged speedily enough but when U Aung Shwe and U Tin U arrived I discovered that U Kyi Maung was not with them. He had been taken away early that morning before dawn. I also discovered that the MI officer had asked them to request me not to leave the house for a few days.

We were given to understand that U Kyi Maung had been taken away to be questioned in connection with the latest student unrest that had erupted in the Rangoon Institute of Technology a couple of days previously. Two students had come to my house on Tuesday and explained to U Kyi Maung what had happened. The authorities were quick to jump to the conclusion that there must be some link between the NLD and the student troubles. This is quite normal. The authorities tend to lay anything that goes awry in the country at the doors of the NLD. We are often amazed at the extent of the influence which the authorities imagine we have upon the course of events within Burma. Their obsession with our organization sometimes reminds us of the words of a song: 'Asleep, my thoughts are of you; awake, my thoughts are of you . . .'

'Business as usual,' we chanted and carried on with our work in the surreal atmosphere of a house arrest that was not a house arrest. We listened to BBC and VOA broadcasts to find out what was going on in the big wide world outside the fence of 54 University Avenue and heard to our surprise that the authorities had claimed I was free to come and go as I pleased. This claim was particularly ludicrous in view of the line of uniformed guards standing at attention in front of the gates of my house. We told our MI officer about this official statement and it was conceded on Friday afternoon that I was in fact free to come and go as I pleased but, of course, I would be 'escorted', which was really nothing new. By that time I had already missed a couple of appointments.

Saturday was the beginning of our annual light festival. Our young people made simple, candle-lit lanterns from bamboo and cellophane in yellow, green, red and blue and that evening and the next, we hung them along the fence. We also let off fire balloons and set off sparklers. Our pyrotechnic activities were of an extremely modest order but there was a certain charm in keeping a traditional festival alive in the midst of restraint.

On the Monday afternoon, U Kyi Maung was released and the road to my house was unblocked. For the time being.

48. Tribute

There is nothing to compare with the courage of ordinary people whose names are unknown and whose sacrifices pass unnoticed. The courage that dares without recognition, without the protection of media attention, is a courage that humbles and inspires and reaffirms our faith in humanity. Such courage I have seen week after week since my release from house arrest fifteen months ago.

Our brave supporters who come to our weekend rallies are a shining symbol of true commitment and strength. There are those who have not missed a single rally and who have become part of the family of our hearts. There is our lovely *Ahmay* ('Mother'), who wears her hair up in an old-fashioned top knot just as my own mother did during the later years of her life. *Ahmay* usually wears an insouciant smile on her face and a small flower in her hair. She is accompanied by *Ahba* ('Father'), gentle of mien and quiet of manners, and by their bright-faced young grandson. *Ahmay* is the centre of a group of democracy faithfuls who have looked the cameras of the Military Intelligence squarely in the lens and again and again braved the threats of the authorities to demonstrate their unwavering support for the cause of democracy in Burma.

These unshakeable stalwarts arrive early in the morning on Saturdays and Sundays and stake out their places in front of my house. They sit against the fence on sheets of newspaper or plastic, seeking respite from the glaring sun under the speckled shade of a tree. During the height of the monsoons, they construct a plastic awning under which they sit out the heaviest deluges with unimpaired spirits and determination. When U Kyi Maung and U Tin U and I come out to speak at four o'clock, they are stationed right in front of the gate with beaming smiles of welcome and affection. They are the representative heart of the thousands who come to our rallies because they believe in the importance of the basic democratic freedoms of association, assembly and expression. They listen intently to what we have to say and respond with intelligence and humour. Time and time again, foreign visitors and correspondents have commented on the extraordinary courtesy and goodwill that is evident among our audience.

Our rallies are political rallies so the main thrust of our speeches is about politics. We respond to letters from the people about the current economic, social and political situation; we discuss the latest international developments; we talk about the struggles for justice and freedom and human rights that have taken place in different parts of the world; we criticize policies and programmes which are detrimental to harmony and progress in the nation; we touch on historical matters.

One could say that each one of the three of us has a 'speciality' of our own. U Tin U, as a one time Chief of Defence Services and Minister of Defence, as one who has spent two years as a monk and as one who has a degree in law, talks most often about matters relating to the armed services, to religion and to the law. He is able to illustrate political truths with stories from the teachings of the Buddha and to analyse actions taken by the authorities against the NLD from the legal point of view. He has an arresting 'voice of command' which at times makes the microphones almost redundant. There is a transparent honesty and sincerity about his words that endear him to the audience.

U Kyi Maung concentrates on economics, history and education and has a delightful sense of humour. Across the road from my house is a compound from which the security services survey my house. During our rallies a video camera team stations itself at the fence and records everything. Around this team there is usually a small group of members of the Military Intelligence and other security personnel: they listen carefully to our speeches and sometimes they laugh so heartily at U Kyi Maung's jokes (some of which are directed against them) that I can see their teeth flashing in their faces. His occasional stories about a 'grandson' with a very MI-like personality are great favourites.

I am the one who responds to letters from the audience and discusses political struggles that have taken place in Burma in the past and also in other parts of the world. I also talk often about the necessity to cultivate the habit of questioning arbitrary orders and to stand firm and united in the face of adversity. One of my most frequent messages is the reminder that neither I alone nor the NLD by itself can achieve democracy for Burma. The people have to be involved in the process, and democracy involves as many responsibilities as rights.

The strength and will to maintain two rallies a week for more than a year came from our staunch audience. At those times when the authorities were at their most threatening, the crowds became larger as a demonstration of solidarity. Even when the authorities blocked off access to my house to prevent the rallies from taking place, the people still came as near as they could to let us and the rest of the world know that they were determined to continue the struggle for the right of free assembly.

49. Operation Anarchy

For some time I have been thinking that I should perhaps, for a change, write a letter about Burmese autumn festivals and flowers, turning my mind from political to cultural and aesthetic interests. But it would not feel right to be quoting verses about scented lotuses under pale strands of moonlight when the political scene is so very unpoetic. So I have to set aside thoughts of the beauty of the dying year and once again focus attention on the current situation in the country.

When I wrote some time ago that life was not dull for dissidents in Burma I did not realize just what an understatement I was making. Something always seems to be cropping up to keep the adrenalin flowing strongly in the NLD system. When we completed our series of meetings at the end of last month, we thought we were in for a period of humdrum administrative work aimed at implementing the resolutions of the meetings. A bit of routine dullness, we thought . . . Such a thought was, of course, tempting fate.

Saturday 9 November. The date should have told us something. There are those who take numerology very seriously and the importance that the authorities in Burma put on the number 9 has become something of a joke, albeit a bad one. The previous weekend, our supporters who had come, very peacefully, as close to my blocked-off road as possible to try to hear me speak had been subjected to harassment by thugs organized by the Union Solidarity and Development Association (USDA) and by members of the security forces. U Kyi Maung, U Tin U and I therefore decided that on Saturday the 9th we would go out of my barricaded road to meet those who had gathered some distance away to demonstrate their support for our cause.

It had been arranged that I would meet U Tin U and U Kyi Maung at the latter's house. I was in a closed car with dark windows to keep out strong sunlight and prying eyes. A blue, closed car which held my MI security personnel led the way and we were followed by a blue open-back van carrying some NLD members and young men from our house and by a black police car. We stayed for about a quarter of an hour at U Kyi Maung's house, then set off for the place where we knew our supporters would be gathered. This time, the blue open-back van was at the head of our motorcade, my car came next, then U Tin U's car which carried both him and U Kyi Maung, then followed the blue MI car and the police car.

U Kyi Maung's house is in a lane off the main road. When we had entered the lane fifteen minutes previously, there had been just a few uniformed members of the security forces and a few people in civilian clothes lounging around the place. But as our cars swung out on to the road, a crowd of people converged on us from both sides. The blue van slipped through unscathed but the mob started attacking our car with stones, iron bars and other lethal instruments under the instructions of a man who had looked in through the front windscreen to check who was inside. In an instant the back windscreen had shattered but fortunately the sunscreen sticker held the pieces together and prevented splinters from scattering over us. There were also two big gashes, probably the result of a flailing iron bar. We continued driving and the whole episode was behind us within a matter of seconds. Later we discovered that U Tin U's car had lost all the glass in both back windows and the back windscreen. The MI escort car also had all its glass shattered and the back windscreen of the police car was in a state comparable to the one in my car.

The most striking feature of the whole episode was that it had taken place within an area which had been cordoned off by members of the security forces, who stood by doing nothing to prevent the attacks. Neither did they make any attempt to arrest the perpetrators of violence. On the contrary, after our cars had driven away, the mob settled down across the road and remained there for several hours under the – one imagines – benevolent eyes of the security personnel.

Where had this mob appeared from? They were members of the

USDA, who had been brought in from the suburbs and satellite townships of Rangoon early in the morning. They were positioned in large groups within the area around my house, which was closed off from the general public to prevent our weekend rallies from taking place.

The attitude of the authorities with regard to the incident is telling. Although there has been an announcement to the effect that an enquiry would be made into the matter, we are not aware that there have been any moves to take action against the thugs, who must be well known to the members of the security forces who had watched them with perfect equanimity as they committed their acts of vandalism. This is in glaring contrast to the zeal with which supporters of the NLD are arrested and condemned to substantial prison sentences for trivial matters. What price law and order in a country where injustice and anarchy are condoned by those who hold official responsibility for protecting the citizens from acts of violence?

50. Respite

Those who have to face persistent political persecution become highly politicized. Our lives take on a rhythm different from those who, on waking up in the morning, do not need to wonder who might have been arrested during the night and what further acts of blatant injustice might be committed against our people later during the day. Our antennae become highly sensitive to vibrations barely noticed by those whose everyday existence is removed from political struggle. But still, our lives are not all politics, we have our personal concerns, our intellectual and cultural interests and our spiritual aspirations. The spiritual dimension becomes particularly important in a struggle in which deeply held convictions and strength of mind are the chief weapons against armed repression.

The majority of the people of Burma are Buddhists and it is traditional for us to gather together on religious occasions to renew our spiritual strength and our ties of friendship. The NLD, like many other organizations in the country, tries to observe major religious festivals. But it is not always easy. The authorities accuse us of using religion for political purposes, perhaps because this is what they themselves are doing, or perhaps because they cannot recognize the multi-dimensional nature of man as a social being. Our right to freedom of worship has become threatened by the desire of the authorities to curtail the activities of our party. This was made particularly obvious in a supplication addressed by the Minister for Religious Affairs to the abbot members of the State *sangha* (community of Buddhist monks) organization on 29 September 1996.

This supplication accused the NLD of infiltrating its party members into various levels of the *sangha* with a view to creating misunderstandings between the government and the *sangha*. It also accused the NLD of instructing its members to enter the religious order to promote the cause of their party and to commit subversive acts (a somewhat baffling statement, that one; it is difficult to see how committing acts of subversion could promote the cause of the NLD). Therefore *sangha* organizations had been 'instructed to contact and cooperate with the relevant state/division, township and ward authorities and take protective measures against dangers to religion'. In other words action should be taken to prevent members of the NLD from entering the ranks of the *sangha*.

It is customary for Burmese Buddhist boys to spend some time as novices in a monastery that they might learn the basic tenets of Buddhism and bring merit to their parents who are responsible for arranging their ordination. In addition, many Burmese men when they have passed the age of twenty enter the religious order again for varying periods of time as fully ordained monks. The supplication of the Minister of Religious Affairs to the State *sangha* organization seemed to be aimed at curtailing the right of members of the NLD to pursue this traditional religious practice. If the authorities truly believe in the accusations levelled against our party in the supplication, they must indeed be out of touch with reality.

But amidst the morass of political repression, intimidation, officially organized acts of anarchy and interference in our right of worship, we gained a brief respite from worldly concerns in the celebration of *kathina*. This ceremony takes place after the end of the rainy season retreat and lasts for one month, from the first day of the waning moon of the month of Thadingyut (this day fell on 28 October this year) until the full moon day of the month of Tazaungdine (25 November). Participation in the *kathina* ceremony, of which the major feature is the offering of new robes, relieves monks of the disciplinary rules to some extent and therefore those donors who arrange the ceremony gain merit.

The NLD made an offering of *kathina* robes at the Panditarama Monastery this year. It was good to gather together to perform a common act of merit. It was good to listen to the discourse of Hsayadaw U Pandita, to ponder over his words of wisdom and to reflect on the meaning of the ceremony. We Burmese believe that those who perform good deeds together will meet again through the cycle of existence, bonded by shared merit. It was good to think that if I am to continue to tread the cycle of existence I shall be doing so in the company of those who have proved to be the truest of friends and companions. Many of us attending the ceremony came together eight years ago to commit ourselves to the cause of democracy and human rights and we have remained together in the face of intense adversity. There were also many missing faces, the ones who had died, the ones who were in prison. It was sad to think of them. But still, it was good to be able to take time off from the political routine, to enjoy a small, precious spiritual respite.

51. A Normal Life

Recently, when a friend asked me how things were with me since the authorities had taken to barricading off my house periodically, I replied that things were fine, I was simply carrying on with my normal life. At this she burst out laughing: 'Yours is not a normal life, in fact it's a most abnormal life!' And I could not help but laugh too.

I suppose the kind of life I lead must seem very strange to some but it is a life to which I have become accustomed and it is really no stranger than a lot of things that go on in Burma today. Sometimes as we walk around the garden while the road outside lies quiet, shut off from the rest of the city, my colleagues and I agree that were we to write about our experiences in the form of a novel it would be criticized as too far-fetched a story, a botched Orwellian tale.

No doubt there are other countries in the world where you would find the equivalent of the huge billboards brazenly entitled 'People's Desire', advertising the following sentiments:

* Oppose those relying on external elements, acting as stooges, holding negative views
* Oppose those trying to jeopardize stability of the State and progress of the nation
* Oppose foreign nations interfering in internal affairs of the State
* Crush all internal and external destructive elements as the common enemy

But I doubt that in other countries you would find just around the corner from such an unwelcoming, xenophobic proclamation, a gigantic, double-faced, particularly unattractive version of a traditional boy doll with puffy white face, staring eyes, a stiff smile and an attaché case (that bit is *not* traditional) welcoming tourists to Visit Myanmar

Year. Bizarre is the word that springs to mind. 'Fascist Disneyland,' one frequent visitor to Burma commented.

There is so much that is beautiful and so much that is wrong in my country. In the evenings when I look out to the lake from my garden, I can see the tattered beauty of the casuarinas, the tropical lushness of the coconut palms, the untidily exotic banana plants and the harshness of the barbed wire fence along the edge of the shore. And across the still waters festooned with clumps of water hyacinths is the mass of a new hotel built with profit rather than elegance in mind. As the sun begins to go down the sky lights up in orange hues. The Burmese refer to this hour as the time of blazing clouds and also as the time when the ugly turn beautiful because the golden light casts a flattering glow on most complexions.

How simple it would be if a mere turn of light could make everything that was ugly beautiful. How wonderful it would be if twilight were a time when we could all lay down the cares of the day and look forward to a tranquil night of well earned rest. But in Fascist Disneyland the velvety night is too often night in the worst sense of the word, a time deprived of light in more ways than one. Even in the capital city of Rangoon, electricity cuts are not infrequent and we are suddenly plunged into darkness. The inability of the government to supply adequate electric power makes it necessary for many households to contrive arrangements of their own, linking up a wire to a neighbouring source that they might enjoy a bit of light at night. The local authorities turn a blind eye to such arrangements, accepting due compensation for their discretion. However, if you happen to be a member of the NLD, trying to bring light into your household can easily result in a two-year prison sentence. The other, and more real, darkness of night in Fascist Disneyland is that so many political arrests are made during the hours when all decent people should be resting and allowing others to rest.

Visitors to my country often speak of the friendliness, the hospitality and the sense of humour of the Burmese. Then they ask how it is possible that a brutal, humourless, authoritarian regime could have emerged from such a people. A comprehensive answer to that question would involve a whole thesis but a short answer might be, as one writer has put it, that Burma is indeed one of those lands of charm and cruelty. I have found more warmth, more wholehearted love, more tenderness, more courage and more caring concern among my people, as we hope together, suffer together and struggle together, than anywhere else in the world. But those who exude hate and vindictiveness and rave about annihilating and crushing us are also Burmese, our own people.

How many can be said to be leading normal lives in a country where there are such deep divisions of heart and mind, where there is neither freedom nor security? When we ask for democracy, all we are asking is that our people should be allowed to live tranquilly under the rule of law, protected by institutions which will guarantee our rights, the rights that will enable us to maintain our human dignity, to heal long festering wounds and to allow love and courage to flourish. Is that such a very unreasonable demand?

52. Year End

This is the last of the weekly *Letters from Burma* series that began in November 1995 and I would like to start it on a note of gratitude. The intervening twelve months since my first letter have been most eventful. There were weeks when so much was happening I could not complete my letter by the agreed deadline. But the Mainichi Shinbun did not once reproach me for my failure to deliver on time; instead, Mr Nagai Hiroshi and other members of the staff demonstrated a fine understanding of the difficulties with which I had to contend. For this understanding, and for the opportunity afforded me to bring the Burmese situation to the attention of the world outside Burma, I would like to express my sincere thanks to the newspaper.

As one deeply involved in the movement for democracy in Burma, it was always my intention to concentrate on the political aspect of life in the country. However, politics is about people and I have sought to bring out the human face of our political struggle. I have written of the effect on ordinary people of such official requirements as the compulsory reporting of overnight visitors to the authorities concerned. I have discussed what inflation means at the common, everyday level of an ordinary breakfast. I have written about friends and colleagues, about the activities of my party, the National League for Democracy, and about the trials, in more than one sense of the word, of political prisoners. I have described traditional festivals and Buddhist ceremonies which are an integral part of life in Burma. I have tried to present politics as multi-faceted and indissolubly linked to social and economic issues.

In recent months I have had to focus increasingly on the challenges the NLD had to face as persecution of its members and supporters reached new heights. The political climate has been very volatile since the end of May when the government took hundreds of NLD Members of Parliament, elected in 1990 but never allowed to exercise their function as representatives of the people, into temporary detention. (There were some whose 'temporary detention for questioning', as the authorities put it, was converted into long prison sentences.) One does not quite know what is going to happen from one day to the next but one can predict that every time the NLD plans a major party activity the government is bound to over-react.

It is not just the activities of our own party that bring down the heavy attention of the authorities upon us. The activities of others also provide them with an excuse for hampering our work. Towards the end of October, students of the Rangoon Institute of Technology staged demonstrations against the way in which some of their numbers had been handled by the municipal police during an incident in a restaurant. As a result, the road to my house was blocked off for the third time within a month (the first two blockades were related to NLD activities) and U Kyi Maung, one of our Deputy Chairmen, was taken in for questioning by the military intelligence. A number of young men who were known to be our staunch supporters were also taken into detention for some days and subjected to severe interrogation.

We have now come to expect that the road to my house will be blocked off late on Friday evening or early on Saturday morning to prevent our weekend public rallies from taking place. The blockade is lifted either on Sunday night or on Monday morning or on Tuesday, as the spirit moves the authorities. On the evening of Sunday 1 December, the road was unblocked and it seemed as though the scene was set for a normal week. But as I observed in one of my letters, 'normal' is not a very appropriate word for describing what goes on in Burma today. When Tuesday morning dawned all seemed as usual, but before 7 a.m. the road had been blocked off once again. And I was prevented from leaving my house. What was it all about? There had been another demonstration led by the students of the Rangoon Institute of Technology. We heard that they were later joined by students from the Rangoon Arts and Science University. Immediately the authorities seemed bent on finding some way of linking this development to the NLD.

The students of Rangoon University established a tradition of social awareness and political activism during the colonial days when they were prominent in the independence movement. The years of authoritarian rule blunted the political awareness of our young people but did not kill the instincts that led them to seek justice and freedom. If there is student discontent, the authorities should seek to redress the ills that lie at the root of this discontent: the protests of the young often reflect the general malaise of their society.

The end of the year is a time for assessing past events and preparing for the future. It is a time for us to decide that we should resolve the problems of our country through political rather than military means.

READ MORE IN PENGUIN

In every corner of the world, on every subject under the sun, Penguin represents quality and variety – the very best in publishing today.

For complete information about books available from Penguin – including Puffins, Penguin Classics and Arkana – and how to order them, write to us at the appropriate address below. Please note that for copyright reasons the selection of books varies from country to country.

In the United Kingdom: Please write to *Dept. EP, Penguin Books Ltd, Bath Road, Harmondsworth, West Drayton, Middlesex UB7 ODA*

In the United States: Please write to *Consumer Sales, Penguin USA, P.O. Box 999, Dept. 17109, Bergenfield, New Jersey 07621-0120*. VISA and MasterCard holders call 1-800-253-6476 to order Penguin titles

In Canada: Please write to *Penguin Books Canada Ltd, 10 Alcorn Avenue, Suite 300, Toronto, Ontario M4V 3B2*

In Australia: Please write to *Penguin Books Australia Ltd, P.O. Box 257, Ringwood, Victoria 3134*

In New Zealand: Please write to *Penguin Books (NZ) Ltd, Private Bag 102902, North Shore Mail Centre, Auckland 10*

In India: Please write to *Penguin Books India Pvt Ltd, 706 Eros Apartments, 56 Nehru Place, New Delhi 110 019*

In the Netherlands: Please write to *Penguin Books Netherlands bv, Postbus 3507, NL-1001 AH Amsterdam*

In Germany: Please write to *Penguin Books Deutschland GmbH, Metzlerstrasse 26, 60594 Frankfurt am Main*

In Spain: Please write to *Penguin Books S. A., Bravo Murillo 19, 1° B, 28015 Madrid*

In Italy: Please write to *Penguin Italia s.r.l., Via Felice Casati 20, I–20124 Milano*

In France: Please write to *Penguin France S. A., 17 rue Lejeune, F–31000 Toulouse*

In Japan: Please write to *Penguin Books Japan, Ishikiribashi Building, 2–5–4, Suido, Bunkyo-ku, Tokyo 112*

In South Africa: Please write to *Longman Penguin Southern Africa (Pty) Ltd, Private Bag X08, Bertsham 2013*